FOREWORD BY
HASSAN AL-HAKEEM

Practical
Advice

10 Guiding Principles to Build
Balance, Happiness & Success

JALAL MOUGHANIA
ABATHAR TAJALDEEN
MOHAMED ALI ALBODAIRI

THE MAINSTAY
FOUNDATION

By: Jalal Moughania, Abathar Tajaldeen, and Mohamed Ali Albodairi

Printed in the United States.

ISBN: 978-1943393077

In the Name of God the Most High

Peace and Blessings be upon the Seal of Prophets

Muhammad and his Holy Household

In dedication to the champions of Karbala

CHAPTERS

FOREWORD

Sayyid Hassan Al-Hakeem

The title of this book speaks volumes about its purpose and objectives. *Practical Advice* is a direct and to the point compilation of practical advice. In its conversational fashion, it speaks to us in a calm and serene tone. It serves as an apt reminder of all the things that we aspire to be.

Practical Advice is an effective practical guide for young Muslims everywhere, especially in North America and Europe. The authors do an excellent job at examining ten crucial characteristics that provide the reader a simplified way to balance living and pursue a happier life. It is rare to find books out there, targeted at the younger generation, written in a way that is casual, conversational, and understandable. Interestingly, the authors tie in the reality that divine leadership and connection to God is alive and well, both implicitly and explicitly, through the Book of God and the Awaited Imam Al-Mahdi (may God hasten his reappearance).

I met the authors eight years ago in Dearborn, Michigan. We have worked together on numerous projects and I can attest to the dedication and sincerity of their work. Each of the authors brings an essential perspective to the table while having the narrations of the Prophet and his Household as well as the verses of the Holy Quran guide the discussion on the essential principles laid out in this book. They are successful in speaking to the reader and relating to the reader because of the relevance of their own backgrounds and experiences.

Practical Advice is a thought provoking and motivational read about how to lead a good life within the framework of Islamic teachings. Throughout its ten chapters, the book weaves insights and life-lessons, along with stories and parables creating an engaging script for a reader of any age. Our community faces numerous challenges. These challenges are most profound for our youth. The youth are constantly met with both internal and external obstacles, trying to find themselves in a world of contradictions. Who am I? What am I? What am I meant to be?

These are questions that young Muslims face every day. And even beyond the deep questions of introspection and identity, they face practical problems and obstacles. How do we balance our school or work life with our family life? How do we look at other people? How does pride and ambition play a role in our character? The authors are able to provide insight and inspiration through this book for the youth that face these types of challenges.

The book is fittingly dedicated to Imam Hussain and his companions who sacrificed their lives on the battlefield of Karbala. As the reader will soon see, there is no shortage of lessons to be learned from this tragedy. Whether it is the Imam himself, his family, or his companions, they set plenty of examples for us to follow in our lives.

For centuries, the commemorations of the events of Karbala have served as gatherings of learning and development. They were never merely ritualistic practices. Rather, through remembrance of the noble characters of that revolution, Muslims have aspired to shape and reform themselves. Along with the brilliant examples of our Immaculate Imams and their companions, the authors weave a set of practical real life examples that are sure to inspire.

Hassan Al-Hakeem
London, UK – February 2019

ACKNOWLEDGMENTS

Our thanks and gratitude is first and foremost to God for His infinite blessings and mercy. Endless thanks for Your endless grace. After that, we would like to thank everyone who helped make this book possible.

Our thanks goes to the Mainstay Foundation and the entire team for helping publish this work. Thank you for making projects like this a reality and emphasizing the importance of talking directly to our youth.

We would like to thank the individuals who reviewed and provided feedback on the book. Thank you for your time, interest, and support.

Thank you to our teachers and mentors. Your work inspires us every day and we are eternally grateful for all that you do.

And to our parents, thank you for raising us to be the individuals we are today. You were behind much of the ideas and experiences expressed in this book.

Finally, we end with our thanks to the Holy Prophet, his Immaculate Household, and the champions of Karbala for providing us the principles we live by. Your sacrifices give us life. Thank you. A thousand times over.

INTRODUCTION

In His Name the Most High

As human beings, compassion is an integral part of our lives. Compassion comes through understanding, through experience, and through contemplation. We see it when we relate to one another, open ourselves to each other's experiences, and reflect on the blessings we have. These blessings are undoubtedly a gift, a mercy, and a token of love from God. That love was manifested in its greatest form by some of God's closest servants – Imam Hussain and his loyal companions 1400 years ago in the land of Karbala. Though seemingly so long ago, their compassionate sacrifice echoes in the undying principles for which they gave their lives. It is out of that love and that compassion that we came together to write this book.

The title of this book is *Practical Advice*. As young adults, we realize the power of ideas. We acknowledge our ability to liberate ourselves by engaging our minds to observe, think, reflect, question and find answers. To liberate our minds, to seek freedom from our own shackles, to move beyond any limitations... that movement towards truly living... towards being. There are many things we strive to be. We selected ten of those things we *should* be and wrote a chapter on each of them. The ten things to be are: free, patient, happy, humble, kind, thoughtful, a friend, real, the change, and extraordinary.

We wrote this book to provide you We wrote this book to share with you the genuine yet practical inspiration that comes from the universal message of Ashura - the day the grandson of the Prophet Muhammad, Imam Hussain, was massacred along with his 72 loyal companions. Beyond being a saga unlike any other, Ashura provides a true education on life. That day alone illustrated key lessons for our benefit even 1400 years later. Lessons in honor, friendship, brotherhood, loyalty, sacrifice, principled-living, and more are a few of the highlights of Ashura - and consequently this book. Ashura is not simply a story of Imam Hussain's death; it is a story of how he lived. In the same light, his sacrifice does not only teach us of the honor that comes with martyrdom but more importantly the sanctity of life.

In this we remember the name of God, *Al-Hayy* – the Living, the Eternal. Through God, we live, breathe, excel, and succeed. He manifests His mercy to us through His messengers and saints; the ones that knew, loved, and honored Him. These messengers and saints were men – humans - like us. But they were the best of us – manifesting God's love and mercy as they were sent to us as the examples to follow and emulate. One of the greatest manifestations of God's love, perfection, and mercy came through the personality of Imam Hussain. He was the ship of salvation and the light of guidance throughout his life, and ultimately manifested the greatest sacrifice through his martyrdom on the lands of Karbala in 680 AD.

It is insightful to look at the words of notable non-Muslim scholars and writers on their perspectives of Imam Hussain. Antoine Bara, a Lebanese Christian writer said, "No battle in the modern and past history of mankind has earned more sympathy and admiration as well as provided more lessons than the martyrdom of Hussain in the battle of Karbala." It's remarkable that not only Muslims, let alone Shia Muslims, have an affiliation to Imam Hussain. It's understandable that Muslims would have an attachment or affinity to Hussain, given that he was an Islamic figure, the grandson of the Prophet of Islam, and one who was widely respected amongst the Arabs of the time. Non-Muslim hearts and minds, that have nothing to do with Islam, are inspired and moved by the tragedy of Karbala.

These individuals wept over him, invigorated by his love and sacrifice, went forward to write and advocate his lessons and teachings. Nonetheless, how does this sacrifice that happened so long ago relate to us? Even if we have made the humble realization that such a tragedy and sacrifice was like no other, and that universities of lessons have sprung from this monumental occasion, how do we implement such lessons? What are the practical, realistic, day-to-day applications of the 7th century tragedy of Hussain into our 21st century lives that show the eternal sacrifice as one that ought not to be ignored or even taken for granted? Essentially, what does Imam Hussain have to give to us? This is what we will answer throughout this book, and you will see that Imam Hussain indeed has much to give. In fact, he has everything to give; we just need to know how to receive it.

As the story of Karbala brings inspiration to all that learn from it, we wholly believe that the benefit the reader will enjoy from this book is measured by the extent of the reader's reflection on such inspiration. We ask you to read these chapters seeking perspective, outlook, insight, betterment, and clarity as a tool for your own development and progress. Let this book be one of reflection and contemplation, just as it was for us as we wrote it. We cannot thank and praise God enough for everything He has given us, and it is, without a doubt, that He has given us *everything*.

One

Be Free

HOW DO WE LIVE FREE?

There are many things that Imam Hussain was known for. He was the pride and joy of his mother Lady Fatima. Imam Hussain's grandfather, Prophet Muhammad, used to play with him every day. The Prophet would sit him on his lap as he taught the Muslims about life, virtue, and excellence. He was the shadow of his father Imam Ali – if it were not for age people could barely differentiate between them. He was the confidant of his brother Imam Hassan and his most trusted advisor. He is known for every virtue: knowledge, bravery, loyalty, leadership, honor, sacrifice, *and freedom*. People call Imam Hussain *Abal-Ahraar*. The Father of the Free, a befitting title for a man who gave every ounce of his being for truth, for justice, for freedom. Imam Hussain sacrificed to preserve our ability to live free, and to knowingly choose our fate in this world *and* the next.

So, let's get right to it. In order for us to live free we need to adopt something called 'balance.' We're not talking about balancing yourself on a thin rope between two buildings as the single escape route for the protagonist of a blockbuster action-packed film that you'd see at the movies. No. So what is this 'balance' we're talking about? Mind you, in any discussion it is essential to define the terms we're using, even on terms that might seem so obvious in their meaning. Why? It's simply because our usage of vocabulary can vary even in the same context. With different intentions, varying understandings of terminology, and distinct perceptions of words due to their connotative or denotative usage, we may think we're all on the same page but later find out that we're reading different books.

Here we will define balance with a key saying by Imam Ali. He says, "Do for this life as if you'll live forever, and do for the next life as if you'll die tomorrow." Balance is to find the middle route in things, to never be extreme, to be steady so that we don't fall one way or another. Imam Ali gives us the equation, the recipe, what we need to live a balanced life – to live a successful life. Imam Mousa Al-Kadhim expands on his grandfather's immaculate saying by advising us to divide our time into four parts.

The first part is strictly devoted to developing your relationship with God, through rituals and acts of worship. This isn't limited to prayer, fasting, and supplication. It can be anything with the clear intention to get closer to God. An example of this would be spending time with a friend who is not feeling well, be it physically or psychologically. If you are spending time with that friend with the intention of being a help, an aid, a support, a shoulder to lean on, in the pursuit of increasing your favor with God because you are being kind to others... that would be worship in itself.

The second part is "going towards earnings." Basically we're talking about working to earn an income. Someone has to work to put food on the table, right? Right. But some people think that if you're religious you can't get rich. If you're religious, you can't be a successful businessman or professional. If you're choosing the path of 'righteousness' you might as well give up on the idea of making money. Wrong. Making money is not bad; it's a great thing actually. The test is what you are going to do with that money. Our Imams don't neglect this reality; in fact, they acknowledge it and mandate working to secure an income for one to support himself and his family.

The Imams inspire us to work and get ahead in life, in everything that we do – not only by getting up and praying on time but by taking care of the rest of our responsibilities as well. We have to make sure that our families are well fed and taken care of. And if that's by going out and getting an education, seeking a professional degree, and getting a professional job – go for it. If it's by becoming a tireless businessman, who pushes his product/service/pitch day-in and day-out, to get where he needs to be – more power to you. The Imams provide us with a holistic approach to living that doesn't neglect a single aspect of building towards success on all levels of our life. The key is in following the guidelines they provide, so that we are able to strike a healthy balance that allows for our optimal growth and success.

The third part is similarly important. The Imam says to spend this time with friends that are trustworthy and sincere. Trust and sincerity are conditions here; the Imam is telling us that they need to have such characteristics in order for this time you spend to be fruitful. It's not just someone who you like to hang out with because they give you a good laugh or tell a good joke. Our friends need to be people of virtue. They need to be people we can learn from. And learning can come in many shapes and sizes. We don't need a particular degree to be a positive inspiration to our friends. By merely setting good examples, by speaking through our actions, and by avoiding hypocrisy, we can teach others volumes of lessons. You don't need to lecture to teach someone about life. All you need to do is be. Be a person of virtue, and surround yourself with virtuous people too. You'll be happy you did. More on friends later though (see chapter 7).

Alright. So, we got the worship down. You're taking care of your ritual obligations. You're praying on time, fasting when you need to fast, and giving charity. Excellent. In addition to your worship, you're taking care of business. Literally. You're making good money and you're working hard. You got this figured out. On top of that, you've chosen your friends wisely and are spending meaningful time with those that are trustworthy and sincere. They help you see your strengths and weaknesses and you do the same for them. We think you're doing pretty well with this checklist. Three out of four are down, now what's the fourth part prescribed by the Imam?

By now you're pretty tired. Let's say you're praying all the time, fasting all the time, working full-time, and sitting with your friends actually takes some time! (pun intended with the 'time'). The fourth part is spending time on 'appropriate pleasures' for yourself. Now you might not be praying, working, and being there for your friends ALL the time, but at the end of the day you need some time to wind down and relax. The Imam is telling us to take that time. After the three parts are met, you should take that time for appropriate pleasures.

Now, what are 'appropriate pleasures'? Essentially, anything that isn't *haram* – forbidden or impermissible or contradictory to the principles and laws laid down by the Quran and the tradition of the Prophet – would be fine. Take this example. It's 9:30pm. You're home after a long day of work. You prayed and took care of all your responsibilities, rituals, family, friends, and the like. Now you want some time just to wind down. You open a bag of your favorite snack, grab a blanket, and pop in one of your favorite movies. Nothing is wrong with that... on its face. If the snack is haram, we got problems here. If the movie is inappropriate, you may have some problems there as well. Nonetheless, keep it clean and consult your jurist if you have questions on Islamic law and its application. Other than that, enjoy the popcorn.

A lot of us may have grown up and been turned off or jaded by religious environments or even religion altogether. These kinds of negative reactions usually come from the misunderstanding or misconception that religion restrains and restricts us unreasonably. That it doesn't allow us to do what we want. It's not foreign to hear things like, "religion is difficult. I feel chained by religion. It pulls me down," and things of the like. That's fine. Many of us go through phases of frustration, questioning, and uncertainty. It really is a learning process. Even when you find yourself in positions of frustration or uncertainty, ask questions and seek the answers. Questioning is not bad; as long as you don't give up and you continue to make the effort.

At least keep an open heart toward understanding religion and the wisdom in its teachings. Tying the fourth part of time back into the discussion, it's critical to realize the importance of this part as an answer to many of the misconceptions of religion being cumbersome, restrictive and unfair. The Imam tells us to take on this fourth part in scheduling your time, so that you strike that balance and are able to successfully perform the rest of your duties and obligations. If you don't give yourself that time to play that game of basketball, go shopping, go to a restaurant, take a walk in the park, etc. it's unlikely that you will be able to strike a balance and reach your optimal potential in all that you do over time.

THINGS CAN GET ANNOYING

We got the four parts of our time down, we have our schedule, and we're ready to go. Awesome. Now what about the unexpected things that come up throughout the day? Those obstacles or annoyances that hit you from left field? How do you deal with those? You just get home and your dad tells you he's working on building a new project in the garage and he wants you to help him. You're tired, stressed with all your work/school, and don't have the time. Your friend gives you a phone call and tells you they really need your help and advice and want you to come over as soon as possible. You honestly don't want to deal with any drama and have enough on your plate as it is. Think of any relevant example that would apply to your life and remember the feeling you get when these things spring up on you.

You start to get anxious, don't you? Even if you feel bad and want to help your dad, or you are feeling empathetic toward your friend, you still get that feeling of anxiousness, nervousness, and being uptight of the possibility of not securing the deadlines or even simple tasks you wanted to do. Big or small, sometimes we just feel like we don't know what to do. One thing we need to keep in mind, throughout this whole reflection of a book, is not to sweat the little things. And when you look at the big picture, most of the things we worry about tend to be little things. Here's an example:

You're driving. If you don't drive because you happen to be too young, or you're simply environment-friendly (hats off to you), you're riding your bicycle. It's a beautiful day with clear skies and little humidity. The birds are chirping, you have your favorite drink in the cup holder, and you're on your way home to have your favorite home-cooked meal. It's a good day...you feel it. Then, all of a sudden, someone cuts you off and slows down, completely catching you off guard, startling you, and spilling your drink! You get upset, furious even. You can't enjoy your drink anymore, the day no longer looks like rainbows and butterflies, and even when you sit down for dinner your favorite meal isn't the same.

Why? Because that inconsiderate driver cut you off and ruined your day! You could probably think of a dozen different examples of small events taking a large toll on our mood and attitude on any given day. Whether it's something said by a complete stranger, the way a coworker handled an assignment, the barista's attitude when you're getting your morning coffee... we allow others to have such a great influence on us, and it's usually in the negative sense. Why do we let others steal our happiness, steal our joy? Why are we going to make such a big deal about things? Why not take a step back and provide reasonable explanations for the events that take place in our day.

With the inconsiderate driver example; do we think about the perspective of that driver? What if he was genuinely in a hurry due to an emergency? Or even more likely, what if he was distracted and honestly didn't see you. We all know that we have days where we aren't completely focused, emergencies spring up on us, or even that we may sometimes unwisely disobey traffic laws simply because we're running late. Things happen. Simply just thinking about it a little more will change our whole perspective. If we just take some time to think about these situations and look beyond our current frustration to see the bigger picture, we realize how small and how very little the things we face really are.

WE NEED TO STRIKE A BALANCE

Another significant issue that we face is striking that balance between the past and present. We find ourselves either so consumed by what we have done in the past or being distracted about what we plan and hope for in the future. We're not saying that thinking about your past is completely useless, nor are we saying that planning for the future is a waste of time. Rather, as you'll see soon, it's all about striking a balance between the two. Any extreme on either end of the spectrum is wrong.

We had a friend; let's say his name was Adam (for the sake of anonymity). Adam used to think and plan so much for everything he was going to do. He decided that straight out of high school he was going to college to pursue a degree in Biomedical Engineering. That summer he planned out every single detail of his Biomedical Engineering degree. He set out to finish his degree in three years, one year earlier than the standard time to complete a Bachelor's degree. How? He said he would increase his course load each semester and take 18 to 21 credits per semester instead of 12 to 15. He outlined what classes he was going to take, in what order, in what semester, with which professor. He had it all down. We were actually kind of jealous that Adam had it all figured out. As soon as he started his first semester, he jumped into planning out his Master's!

So he set out to plan all of his courses, with which professors, and which semesters for his newly found interest in completing a Master's degree. This was all before the end of his first semester. His friends tried to advise him otherwise, but he was adamant that he had to plan for the future. Adam's performance in the classroom suffered, he was stressed out, his family was worried about him, and he just was overall bent out of shape. Adam didn't see what his problem was until he heard his father relay the words of Imam Ali when he said, "Do for this life as if you'll live forever, and do for the next life as if you'll die tomorrow."

Adam thought he was doing what was best for himself by planning ahead and keeping his eyes on the 'prize.' But what really is the prize? A degree? A job? That dream house with your dream car parked in the driveway? None of those things bring you happiness. Because that's essentially the goal: to be happy. The key to happiness is being able to truly balance between one's short term and long term goals, all the while being aware of what the goals are to begin with and actually accomplishing them through the right means.

Consider the words of the Holy Quran where God tells people, "This worldly life is not but diversion and amusement; and indeed the home of the hereafter is the eternal life, if only they knew."[1] How do you take that and think about your short term and long term goals? You have a lot of things going on in life. We all do. But you can't let that make you lose sight of the big picture and what's to come – the hereafter. What we do here, what we do in this life, is going to be a mirror – a reflection – of what you are going to see in the afterlife. So in order to see something good in the afterlife, you better make sure you have something pretty to look at. Obviously we're not talking about makeup. But take the example of makeup. If a young lady were to put on makeup in the dark, and she's unskilled at the task to begin with, do you think she's going to see a pretty sight once she flips on the switch and looks in the mirror?

Back to goals and the big picture. You have to look at things in both the short term and the long term. You can't neglect either. The key in short-term and long-term goal setting is prioritization. You need to ask yourself, 'what's important?' And given the fact that we don't actually have all the time in the world, you have to ask yourself, 'what's urgent?' Importance and urgency are two very important measures in setting and prioritizing goals.

---

[1] The Holy Quran, 29:64.

If you want to be effective with your time and achieving your goals, write down all the things you need and want to do. Yes, write them down on a piece of paper. Open up a text box on your laptop, or even a note on your cellphone. Whatever the tool or medium, just get it out of your head and onto that thing in front of you. List them as they come to mind. Once you're done listing all of them, then re-organize and categorize based on importance and urgency. It may seem tasking or annoying at first, but you'll get the hang of it and see how helpful it actually is.

Don't fall into the classic thought that you'll get things done together at the same time, something many of us call 'multi-tasking.' Multi-tasking is just a fancy way of saying, "I'm not focused." Don't get us wrong, some people are actually able to do multiple tasks at once and effectively get things done. But, those who are able to do so and be effective are very rare.

Challenge accepted! No. Please. Do not take this as a challenge. Many of us have gone down this road and still suffer from this condition – it's not good news. Take our advice and just do things one at a time.

BE FLEXIBLE BECAUSE PEOPLE MATTER

It is great to be a planner. There are many benefits in planning ahead, and being a planner is a great characteristics to have. You naturally get yourself to identify your goals and work out a way to accomplish them. But sometimes planning can make us uncompromising and even stubborn. Life can throw you some curveballs and you need to know when and how to adapt to the changes that you face. So be flexible with your plans. This can especially apply to those of us who are older but still young enough to be youthfully ambitious.

Take the example of Adam and Ali. In their semesters together in grad school they were studying in the library. An idea for a new project hit Ali. While Adam was deep in study mode, and Ali seemingly looked like he was studying, Ali pitched the idea to Adam. "Sounds cool, but let's talk about it later Ali." Ali replies, "Hey it's only going to take fifteen minutes. I just have to get it out there and bounce back some ideas." In that situation, Adam conceded and they had their discussion about this new project. He was flexible because he saw the sincerity in Ali's tone and realized that what he had to talk about was important to him. Mind you there are times where Adam would not concede and would simply move to the other side of the library because he wanted to ace his exams. The point here is that people matter.

We may have time set aside specifically for certain things that cannot be interrupted, and often that time should not be disrupted. Examples include work, class, studying, etc. But we are human at the end of the day. And though it is so important for us to be considerate and not interrupt one another, sometimes it happens. When we are interrupted how do we react? Are we benevolent and kind, or are we rigid and unforgiving? Try giving someone those 10 or 15 minutes they need to talk or to help them with a favor. It may not mean much to you, but it will mean the world to them could really make a world of a difference.

ARE MATERIAL THINGS BAD?

Now when we looked at the things we have, and considering the discussion of short-term and long-term goals, how does our material life affect us? The clothes we wear, the house we live in, the car we drive, the games we play, the things that are material. How do these things play a role in our life? We all like nice things because nice things are... nice, right? We strive to get great jobs to make money. We use that money to buy ourselves nice cars and nice clothes. We move in to bigger and newer houses and take more vacations. In doing these things we feel we are being accomplished. But are these really accomplishments in their own right? Are these meaningful accomplishments?

What is an accomplishment of a high school student? Getting a great GPA. How about a college student? Doing well enough to get accepted into a graduate program. You get into your graduate school – law, medicine, business, pharmacy, humanities, etc. You graduate and land a great job. You make a lot of money and have an impressive reputation in the field you work in. These are accomplishments are praise-worthy; there is no doubt about it. As long as you have a noble cause in mind for achieving such goals, like supporting your family and seeking financial stability and independence for your own integrity and your family's dignity, these are great successes. But what is key here is that we do not limit our definition of accomplishments simply to things that bring material gain. Our vision of achievement and success should be broader than what society may carve out for us in the typical molds of wealth, fame, and influence. So what are accomplishments that we can strive for that are not material?

On his way to a work meeting one day, Hassan realized that the time of prayer had hit. Hassan decided that he would quickly pray and continue on his way. He was running late and naturally was in a hurry. He did his *wudoo'* (ritual washing before prayer) and put out his rug and started praying. When he finished he realized that he barely affected the time he was expecting to arrive at the program. How you may ask? Well it wasn't a miraculous feat of spirituality that stopped time, that's for certain. Rather, he realized that he finished his prayers in less than 3 minutes. That is pretty fast. So he asked himself, "How much am I putting into my prayer?" It made him think long and hard. "It continues to be a question I struggle with," he says. "If I am not putting much into my prayers to God, then why should I expect much in return? This is a time when we are meeting God; we are actually having a conversation with our Creator. Why don't I take the time to talk to Him?" How many of us think about it like that?

The Holy Prophet said, "Prayer is the pillar of faith." Look at any structure, any building, and you will see that most buildings are held up by pillars. Some are decorative and shown, others are hidden, but they all serve the purpose of holding the building together. Prayer is the same way. Prayer is the foundation that religion and faith are built on. So how much time do we put into our prayer? The narrations from the Ahlulbayt tell us that we get out of our prayers what we put into them. If we put in the time, we could possibly claim a success that is unmatched.

Other than our prayers, how about tending to our parents and our families? Being a good son or daughter is possibly one of the greatest accomplishments one could attain. Though we would all like to think of ourselves as blessings to our parents, sometimes we are not. Sometimes we are simply a burden. Now think about that for a few moments. These are the individuals that brought us into this life and nurtured us for years, even in the most basic of ways. How do we repay them? How do we show our gratitude and appreciation for the sacrifices they made for us? The money, the time, the sleep, and so many things they sacrificed just to bring you into being. The very thought is awe-inspiring. We need to show our appreciation and gratitude to our parents because we are truly indebted to them.

Take a look at the words of Imam Ali Al-Sajjad, our fourth Imam, in his Treatise on Rights. On the rights of your mother, he says,

> *The right of your mother is that you know that she carried you where no one carries anyone, she gave to you of the fruit of her heart that which no one gives to anyone, and she protected you with all her organs. She did not care if she went hungry as long as you ate, if she was thirsty as long as you drank, if she was naked as long as you were clothed, if she was in the sun as long as you were in the shade. She gave up sleep for your sake, she protected you from heat and cold, all in order that you might belong to her. You will not be able to show her gratitude, unless through God's help and giving success.[2]*

Don't forget your father.

> *The right of your father is that you know that he is your root. Without him, you would not be. Whenev-*

---

[2] Imam Ali Al-Sajjad. Treatise on Rights. Right 22: The Right of the Mother.

> *er you see anything in yourself which pleases you,*
> *know that your father is the root of its blessing up-*
> *on you. So praise God and thank Him in that meas-*
> *ure. And there is no strength save in God.*[3]

Another non-material success that we can strive for is helping people – even if it is in the simplest of ways. Being there for a friend when they call you and ask for a favor. Help an old woman cross the street. Spare some change for a homeless man on the road. Get in the habit of asking people if they actually need help. Sometimes our pride may inhibit us from reaching out to others for help but we really need a friend to give a lending hand. Don't wait for people to ask, be there when they need you. If you are able to achieve that, you will be in a good place.

If you are serious and ambitious about attaining this kind of success, consider sponsoring an orphan. With a very small contribution you can change someone's life. Many charitable organizations for orphans ask generous donors for as little as $25 a month, which in some countries covers the orphan's needs for food, shelter, and education. Imagine that. With the amount that is less than a monthly gym membership and barely enough to cover a dinner for two, you can take care of an orphan. You would contribute to this orphan's health and safety. You would be the helping hand that made a difference in that child's life. If that isn't success we're not sure what

---

[3] Imam Ali Al-Sajjad. Treatise on Rights. Right 23: The Right of the Father.

is. You see, it is in these things that we have a sense of fulfillment and purpose and a way to true happiness. We want to be successful because we want to be happy. But material things don't make us happy, it is our sense of purpose and our ability to make a positive difference in life that does.

When we think of the tragedies that took place on the Day of Ashura in Karbala, we remember the many children that were orphaned that day. We think of these innocent children who had to witness the gruesome massacre of their fathers, their uncles, and their brothers. When we remember their tragedies and honor their sorrow, we realize how blessed we are to have our parents and children with us today. We need to remind ourselves of how blessed we are and articulate our appreciation of these blessings to those around us, and ultimately to God who keeps His doors of mercy open to us.

WHAT SETS US APART?

After covering these past crucial points, we want you to ask yourself an important question: what sets us all apart? Is it our jobs and the fields we work in? Or is it the kind of house we live in and the place in which we reside? Is it the money in our bank accounts and the technology we have? Or is it family we belong to and the names we carry? Some of these things are material and some of them are not. These things do not really set us apart. What sets us apart is what we do with these things that we have. It's not bad to have material things, nor is it bad to have great non-material things like family and friends. But it is what we do with these things and these relationships that determines what kind of people we are.

Think about everything that you have. We find ourselves praying for God to bless us in this life and the next. This is a prophetic tradition. There is nothing wrong to be blessed in this life, with both material and non-material things. But the key question is whether I am pleasing God with what He has blessed me or not? Are these things a means for me to get closer to Heaven or Hell – Heaven being the eternal pleasure of God and Hell being God's displeasure and damnation.

At the end, we want you to remember something that is key for our success and happiness, "An hour of contemplation is worth 70 years of worship." – Prophet Muhammad. Reflection is the key for our success, in this life and the next.

Two

Be Patient

PATIENCE IS A VIRTUE

When we look at the stories of our Prophets and Imams we see a continuous theme of excellence in their characters. They were the best people to walk this Earth. They showed us the ropes and how to live our own lives. They sacrificed so that we may learn, appreciate, and know how to handle our own challenges and hardships. One thing they continued to utilize throughout their lives was the virtue of patience. After all, life is only test. Acknowledging this reality, think of this question when reading this chapter: in the test of life, what kind of student are you?

Think of the name of God, *Al-Sabour* – the Patient. God's representatives on Earth – the ones He chose to guide humanity – manifest His attributes and His will. One of the attributes that is especially found in our prophets and imams is the attribute of patience. From God's first prophet, Adam, to His last vicegerent on Earth, Imam Al-Mahdi, God's ambassadors were the best examples of patience and forbearance. Just think of Imam Al-Mahdi, who has been waiting for over a thousand years for his followers to be ready. There is a misreading that some of us tend to have, which is that we are waiting for the Imam to return. Yes, we may in fact be waiting for his return but we are not prepared or ready for his return. He is ready, he is prepared, he is waiting to reappear and come forth past the clouds that veil us from him. Waiting would entail readiness but until we are ready we can't say that we are truly waiting. He is ready. He is waiting. He is waiting for us to be ready. It is as simple as that.

Now think of how hard it is on the heart of this Imam of ours, that he has waited for over a thousand years and still his followers are not ready for him, let alone the rest of humanity. The Awaited Imam is a living testament to what patience is and the best example of what it means to be patient through the strength of conviction in principle and faith. Following the example of God's prophets and vicegerents, we know that patience is the tool to taking on life's tests successfully. Keep the thought of the Imam with you as you read the rest of this chapter.

Think of the student that comes to school one day and gets surprised with the infamous pop quiz. He's not prepared for it, he's been spending practically all of his time working on a final project for another class. Or consider the employee that is falling behind at work and struggling to keep up with deadlines getting assigned a new project by his manager. He barely knows how he is going to deliver on the previous deadlines and this new project just seems impossible. Finally, the family scene – a mother goes home after a long day of work and is expected to solve everyone else's problems. Dinner isn't cooked, the house is a mess, the kids need help with their homework, and her 13-year old daughter is way over due for a 'birds and the bees talk.' You would think patience would be required here to maintain some sanity, right? Absolutely. So what do we do? We need some guidance, some help, some instructions and even inspiration when we face our day-to-day challenges.

Whenever we contemplate topics like this we are bound to go back to the Holy Quran – the Word of God – to derive inspiration and guidance. On patience, God tells us, "Do the people suppose that they will be let off because they say, 'We have faith,' and they will not be tested?"[4] This verse sums it all up for us. Basically, if we really want to be Muslims – believers in God – we have to do more than just talk the talk. We need to talk the talk, walk the walk, and possibly even pick up some chalk to illustrate to others (i.e. our siblings, children, family and friends) how to navigate problems through conviction on the metaphorical blackboard of life. See that was not merely a bad rhyme; there was purpose in the chalk.

God is telling us that if we truly mean what we say, that 'we have faith,' we are going to be tested. It's as simple as that. Take the example of a college course,

---

[4] The Holy Quran, 29:2.

or even think back to high school when courses were assigned for you. Did you ever walk into a classroom thinking that you would go through the course without taking a single quiz, test, or some form of evaluation? Some of us may have breezed through 'blow-off' classes, but there was always a test. Even a high school gym class, one of the most fun classes for some of us, had tests. Beyond the mere fact that we will get tested, the outcome of the test is an indicator of how much we know about what we are being tested on. If you know your geography you will do well on your geography exam. If you practiced your 2-mile run, you will likely pass your fitness test. If you are conscious of the way this world works and are aware of God's mercy and blessings, you will likely do well with the tests and trials you face in this life. What is great about our tests and trials in this life is that, contrary to the grading of some professors in college, effort actually does count towards your 'grade.' God rewards us for our good intentions and for the efforts we put forward.

TRIALS AND FAITH

We are tested every day and we will continue to be tested until the last breath we take. Our Imams tell us that there is a direct relationship between these tests and the level of our faith. Our sixth imam, Imam Jafar Al-Sadiq, said, "The most tried are the prophets and the infallibles, then the people per their strength in their faith." If you are a 'man of faith' or a 'woman of faith,' you are an individual who practices patience. You are an individual who faces so many problems but are able to stand resilient in the face of that adversity and say, 'alhamdulillah' – praise be to God. You are a person that no matter what happens, you can still smile – following the example of our Holy Prophet.

The Prophet was known for his smile, a smile so resilient that even his enemies were greeted by it. When the Prophet used to walk outside he would be greeted by an old woman who would conveniently be taking out her trash. She wouldn't place her trash on the curb like you and I may do every Monday or Tuesday morning. She would make the deliberate effort to throw piles of trash at the Prophet every time he crossed by. What would the Prophet do? Would he throw the trash back or give a nasty look like many of us would naturally be inclined to do? Far from it, the Prophet would only respond with his brilliant smile and simply carry on. One day, the Prophet walked that same path but was surprised not to see the trash-throwing woman like he usually did. You would think, 'what a relief!' Instead, our Prophet was concerned. He was concerned for her well-being. He inquired about her health. He would find her ill in her home, alone, unable to care for herself. So, the Prophet took it upon himself to care for her, to feed her, to get her medication and sit at her bedside providing her the warmest of company. The Holy Prophet, in that moment alone, and there are many more like this, showed us the pinnacle of excellence in virtue and ethics – the best example of faith in God and practice of patience.

When we strive to achieve anything in life, we find that the greater the achievement the greater the adversity in getting there. You want to become a physician so that you can be part of the noble cause of saving people's lives. A beautiful aim, but it requires you to do a few things. You need to get admitted into a university and earn a bachelor's degree. While completing your bachelors, which normally takes four years, you also need to take the MCAT and apply to medical school. Once you get admitted to medical school you have another four years of rigorous study. Those four years are followed by tests, the infamous boards exams, and residency programs that typically take three years to complete. If you would like to specialize in a certain field of medicine, you would naturally add a couple more years to be certified in your field of specialty. So after graduating high school, you're looking at a good 10+ years of education to be able to practice medicine. If you want to be accomplished and deserve the title you strive for, you will be tested. It is the same with faith.

CHALLENGES ARE OPPORTUNITIES

Anyone that has played in organized sports – from football and soccer to basketball and baseball – knows that you need to work hard to play hard. You need to put in the effort to see results. I remember when I played soccer in high school our coach stressed the most on conditioning. He did not spare a moment for us to rest. He utilized every moment in practice to push us forward, maximize our results and reach our potential. "Keep going! You can do this, don't give up! You're stronger than that," he would scream at us at the top of his lungs. It motivated us, made us feel that we could endure and persevere. And we saw results. We pushed ourselves because we knew that if we pushed harder, gave more effort, we would only get better. Our resolve was constantly examined. Our patience was tested. We welcomed the test. Why? Because we were proof of the principle. When we prepared and pushed forward, knowing what we were being tested for, we excelled – we became better and got closer to our potential.

Apply that same vigor and struggle for excellence, to your relationship with God. In order to progress you need to have your goals in mind, you need to be thinking about what you want to accomplish and where you want to be. If we are not even thinking about God in our actions and our daily functions, what kind of progress could we realistically expect from ourselves? If God is not in our active thoughts, if what He expects and wants for us does not even cross our minds then where are we on our personal scales of excellence? Where are we in our own spiritual and intellectual fitness? We're far off.

But that does not mean we cannot pick ourselves up, get back into conditioning and make the most out of the season we are in. Don't wait until next season. Make the necessary changes now. You have the tools at your disposal and you have the best mentors and the best coaches – the Holy Quran and the Ahlulbayt. Use what you have and push yourself forward, because your potential is immeasurable. Keep the priceless words of inspiration by Imam Ali with you, especially when you need the push to be patient, to become better, to excel and be resilient. He says, "You think that you are insignificant, but within you lies the greater universe."

These are practical examples of how we are challenged and tested and we must apply their lessons to our relationship with God and our ultimate test in this life before we move on to the hereafter. But one question remains. Even though teachers have a good sense of the progress of students by mere interaction and student participation, they still need the confirmation of examination to test the student's grasp and knowledge of the subject matter. In other words, we take tests to show how well we know our stuff. When it comes to God, He knows everything so He is fully aware of what we know, how well we know it, and where we are in our progress. So why does He test us, if He already knows how we are doing? In fact, He knows how we will do even before we actually do it – God's knowledge encompasses all that was and will be. He created the system and all the infinite options within it. He knows His creation better than the creation knows itself. So why test us if He already knows the test score?

Imagine if God were to send us to Heaven or Hell without giving us the opportunity to prove our worthiness and manifest our decisions into our own reality? We fast-forward to Judgment Day and there we are being sent to Heaven or Hell one after the other. Those of us who would be given Heaven might not complain because of the blessing they'll be in. But those who are sent to Hell will definitely ask God why they were punished when they did not carry out the actions that would deserve punishment. "This isn't fair! I didn't do any of these things that I'm being punished for." You're right it wouldn't be fair. And that is essentially why God willed for this life to play out as it does in providing people opportunities to make their own choices, even though He already knows the outcome. Because of God's mercy He gives us the free will as opportunity to be challenged and to make the right choices, or the wrong ones.

Even though He knows, He gives us the test for this life so we know for ourselves. He challenges us as an opportunity for us to prove ourselves and show what we are worth. Our free will, our freedom to choose our fate, our liberty to manifest our own destiny is a daunting responsibility but the greatest blessing. That blessing is a testament of God's mercy and beneficence.

PREDESTINATION OR FREE WILL?

People ask this question all the time and mistakenly interpret God's all encompassing knowledge to mean that we are predestined to do the things that we do and have no real control over our actions. That is false. In our realm, we have the freedom to choose and make decisions that dictate how our future will unfold.

Imagine a seven-year-old boy running around the house holding the glass of milk his mother just gave him. Because he was fooling around he managed to spill milk all over his mother's carpet. After his mother scolds him he simply replies, "Mom, it's not my fault. I'm really not responsible. This was destined to happen. In reality I have no control over this situation so I can't be blamed and thus I shouldn't be punished." Beyond being astonished at her son's eloquence, do you think the mother will buy her son's argument? Of course not. Well, we hope not at least. "No darling it doesn't quite work like that. You see, you chose to take the glass of milk from me and run around the house. You know how the combination of those two actions works out. I've warned you against it before. You made a choice. You were aware and now you are responsible. Sorry buster, but you're grounded," says the mother schooling her quick-witted child. Most of the time the apple doesn't fall far from the tree.

Interestingly enough, that same 'logic' was used by the people that killed Imam Hussain. They said, "It was God's will. He meant it to happen. I don't have control. God is in control." Is this something that we accept in our faith? Do we have this line of thinking as part of the religion? Or is it simply a scapegoat for people who commit crimes, large or small, to justify their actions?

We believe that every single individual is responsible for his or her actions. What you are doing now, what you will be doing tomorrow, and what you did yesterday, you are responsible for and accountable.

But God knows everything that is going to happen. Sometimes we try to bring God down to our level, applying him to our world, so that we can understand him. But by doing that all we are doing is limiting God in our minds. And when you put any form of limit on God you have absolutely misunderstood Him, because His very essence is limitless. When we misunderstand God we are not only doing injustice to Him, we are doing the greatest injustice to ourselves. Instead of bringing God down to our level we need to elevate ourselves to understand Him. God is beyond time, matter and space. Once we liberate our minds beyond the confines of our own limitations we can at least appreciate the blessed fact that God is so magnanimous. He is like nothing else.

So in all of this, we need to take a step back and realize what a blessing the entire system that God created for us is. All the tests, trials and tribulations we face are opportunities for us to prove our worth. God does not need to try us, but He does so simply out of His mercy for us; giving us opportunities to realize our true potential and reach it. He wants us to excel and better ourselves. None of this is in vain. The purpose is excellence and the mechanism towards that is this life filled with tests that are our opportunities to realize our success.

Trials are Positive

God says in the Holy Quran, "And We shall give to them a taste of the lesser suffering before the greater suffering so that they may return."[5] So that we may return to what? So that we may return to our senses. So that we may return to our reflection. So that we may return to the path of God and His Prophet. God gives us a taste of suffering in this world, like a disease or illness. You wake up one morning and you're so sick and weak that you can't get out of bed. What does that do to you? Beyond what you're experiencing physically, what does that do to you psychologically, emotionally, and spiritually? Do you become disgruntled, upset, depressed? Or are you grateful for this reminder that one day you won't be alive anymore and if you don't make the most of this life your hereafter will be a lot more unpleasant than the flu you're struggling with? How do you deal with these situations?

We have a good friend that taught us the importance of having a positive perspective and that every situation, especially trials, is an opportunity to learn and be humble. Our friend, let's call him Gabriel just for the sake of anonymity, is a real stand up guy. Gabriel is hardworking and in top physical condition. A few years back Gabriel discovered that he had a few

---

[5] The Holy Quran, 32:21.

slipped disks in his back. Every once in a while he has an episode where his back completely gives out and he is unable to walk or even stand. Not too long ago, he had an episode. It was at about 8:30 am, right before he was heading out to work. His back gave out and he fell to the floor. In the excruciating pain, he yelled, he screamed, he cried in agony. His wife and kids were not home, they were at work and school. No one was there. No one could hear him. He had to crawl around the house on his stomach because any move he would make could be devastating. Why didn't Gabriel call for help, one of us possibly, one of his close friends or family? "One, I didn't want anyone to see me like that. But even more so," Gabriel said, "is that I reflected in that position more than I ever have. I realized how little and weak we are. Without God we are nothing. A little nerve can cripple me to the ground, weak and helpless. Without Him we're nothing."

We get these smaller, lesser sufferings so that we can realize before the greater sufferings come. Another enlightening experience like this takes place when we attend a funeral. Death is the greatest reminder for us and one of the most direct stimulators for reflection and contemplation. When we remember death, it is one of the few times that our hearts, minds and spirits gravitate back to God in His remembrance. We have a collective affinity in the undeniable reality of "We are for God and to Him we shall return." Illness and death are truly lesser sufferings when compared to what could be the fate of a person who is immoral, cruel, or tyrannical in this life. But more examples could include even simpler or practical things like getting a flat tire, failing an exam, or getting demoted at work. They all can devastate us or make us realize that life is greater than those mere trials. With every triumph we become more prepared for the true tests to come.

THE CIRCLE OF LIFE

"If a wound has afflicted you a wound like it has also afflicted the people; and We bring these days to men by turns, and that Allah may know those who believe and take witnesses from among you; and Allah does not love the unjust."[6] You may be feeling pain, you're feeling upset, mad, sad, down, depressed. Know that you're not alone. People have gone through and are going through the same things you are experiencing now. Our experiences are not absolutely unique, we all share in the challenges, tests and trials of life. You got a bad grade on your senior project in college, you didn't get accepted into law school, you lost your job, you got a divorce.... All of these experiences have been had by other people.

---

[6] The Holy Quran, 3:140.

Rest assured that you are not the first and you won't be the last.

In addition to that, instead of moping over how bad the situation is think about how much worse it could be and how much better you have it than others. You didn't get that scholarship you wanted, but at least you're still going to college. They didn't offer you the job you've been dying for, but at least you still have your degree. You are stressed out and depressed because you can't find a job after getting laid off, but at least you still have a roof over your head and food on the table. There are people that are starved, orphaned, killed every day, not only in a specific country or region but across the world and in our own neighborhoods and cities. All the while, we complain about why our phones are not updating.

If we are appreciative of all that we have and realize that these 'tests' are really blessings in disguise, we would conquer the world with our smiles and positive energy. We would realize that we really shouldn't sweat the small stuff and when it comes right down to it, it's all small stuff. Take a minute to think back to Imam Hussain who died and sacrificed himself 1400 years ago. We look back at his tragedy and say, "What a man. What a hero. What a legend. This man gave everything so that you and I can be something." He gave everything so that we can be reminded year after year what life is really about. Because of him we know that it is so much more than what it often seems to be, it's so much more.

When we look at social media sites and platforms nowadays we often see the common sentiments of negativity held by teenagers. "I hate my life," or "Life sucks," or the simple abbreviations like "FML" are all too common. But why? To all the teens out there, read carefully. You are young, beautiful, energetic, creative, and full of potential. Don't throw away the blessings you have by being thankless. You have the whole world before you and, God willing, a whole life ahead of you. If you feel down or depressed, change your atmosphere. Get up, take a walk, pick up a pen, write, draw, read, do something. Do not let yourself sour into boredom. There is too much life out there and too much life in you to let yourself be 'bored.' Use the time you have in your youth to make your future even better. Think ahead, plan ahead, and get ahead. Take advantage of the time you have because time runs out and it is only followed by real sorrow and regret if it is wasted. Don't throw it away so easily.

As we get older we realize even more the concept of the circle of life. One day we can be on top of the mountain and everything is flowing and streaming perfectly for us. Everything seems to be working out, so much so that even things that we are not anticipating fall into place and play in our favor. We hopefully say, *alhamdulillah* – praise and thanks be to God – and move forward with the blessings, appreciative and thankful. On another day though, it can be the extreme opposite. We fall to the lowest point of the valley and everything is flowing against us. During the economic recession that the nation experienced in 2008, so many families lost everything they had within just a few months - their home, their car, their job, their savings, almost everything. Within the blink of an eye everything can be stripped from us. These experiences humble us. Even if we haven't gone through them ourselves, we can look at others' experiences and learn that it doesn't matter so much if we are on top of the mountain or at the bottom of the valley. It matters what we do with our situation. What sort of inner peace we create for ourselves through the contentment which God has given us.

A few summers ago Ali was moving some patio furniture at his parent's house. One of the accent tables had a glass top. As he was carrying it, the glass top fell and shattered across the pavement. He was devastated. No, he really wasn't but he did have to clean it up. Think about that shattered glass. One day it was perfectly fine and the next day it was shattered and had to be thrown away. Instead of killing yourself over the broken glass, all you have to do is clean it up and replace it. That's exactly what Ali did. Thirty dollars and a day later, voilà, good as new! Don't devastate yourself over the small things. Look at the bigger picture and keep on moving forward. When you utilize these small pieces of advice you'll become less anxious. You won't be as stressed out as often. Your family will like you more because you won't be making as much of a big deal of things as usual.

PATIENCE IS KEY

No matter how much you talk about enduring trials and tribulations and understanding this 'circle of life,' if you don't have this one component you won't be able to actually endure and overcome your trials and tribulations. That component is called patience. If you don't have patience, life is basically going to suck for you.

Okay. We get it. We have to be patient, fair enough. But how do we be patient? It is said so often and repeated so many times. "Be patient," "Patience is a virtue," "Patience!" It's very simple, but it's difficult. *Practice.*

A lot of us are not good at being patient. So how do we get better at something that we are not good at? We have to practice. It's as simple as that. You don't know how to ride a bike, how do you learn? You practice. You want to try out for the basketball team but your skills are not where they need to be for you to be competitive. What do you do? You live night and day at the basketball court and practice. Better yet you practice and practice with people that are better than you at the sport itself. So hang around people that are good at what you want to be good at. If we hang around people that have nothing to do with patience, do you think it'll help us become more patient? Not at all. In the next chapters, we will talk more about friends and how big of a role they play in our growth and development. But know one thing in summary; friends can make or break you. They can help you grow or they can take you down to places that you never thought you would stoop so low.

If you have a group of people around you that are not patient and every time someone tells them something they just blow up, you're setting yourself up for failure. Even on an individual level, independent of friends, there are things that we can do to practice our patience. If someone or something agitates you, you need to change the situation you are in before you react in a way that you will regret. Changing the situation could be as simple as changing your physical position. Imam Ali advises us to change our position if we get angry or upset. If you're standing then sit down. If you are sitting then get up and take a walk, or remain in place but lay down. Take a nap, go to sleep. Change. The point is to take control of the situation. We are responsible for our actions. Each individual is accountable for his or her choices and behavior – not anyone or anything else.

SATAN MADE ME DO IT

Please be especially mindful that people who say that the 'Shaitan', Satan, made them do it are very wrong. A young man named Jamal made the mistake of thinking this way. Jamal was a professional. Ironically he was an account manager at an ad-agency. At the same time he was a big gambler. He tried stopping his bad gambling habits but didn't try hard enough. On one December night in 2013, he decided to go to the casino downtown. He was feeling lucky. After 4 hours at the casino, however, Jamal didn't turn out to be so lucky. He managed to lose more than $200,000 in his four-hour sitting, effectively breaking the bank. Jamal had a wife and three kids. Even though he had a well-paying job he struggled to pay his mortgage, his car payment, and even put food on the table. The $200k from the December night was not the only amount of money he lost; he owed another $75k from a previous gambling rendezvous. He tried to hide it from his family but his wife figured it out. She knew about his problem. She tried helping him before. But this time it was way too much. She left him and took the kids to their grandparents' house. Because things kept piling up and he became more and more distracted he eventually lost his job months later for lack of productivity at the workplace. He managed to ruin everything. When a close friend asked, "What happened to you?" Jamal answered, "It was the Shaitan man. He took control of me." His friend would sigh and say, "He didn't need to. You're your own devil my friend."

Jamal's conclusion was misguided. Satan has no control over us. He never did and he never will. The Holy Quran clearly tells us that the only ability he has is to whisper – to suggest, promote, advertise. When you see billboards for expensive cars, clothing or perfumes that push you even more to wanting to buy the product, is that ad-agency controlling you to make a detour and take the exit for the store? They wish they had that control over you, though their power of suggestion is sometimes very close to it. But that's what it is – the power of suggestion. And that is what it will only be. The difference is how much you and I allow that suggestion to affect our decision-making. Satan is in the business of marketing and advertisement - he's one of the best actually. But that does not mean he has any power over us. We have the power to resist. We have the ability to choose what's right and ignore the suggestions, the promotions, the advertisements. It may be difficult but it is very simple. We just have to know that we are in control and not fool ourselves otherwise.

THE SOLUTION IS IN PATIENCE

"Patience in one's life is similar to that of the head to the body. If the head leaves the body, the body becomes useless and dysfunctional. Thus, if one cannot become patient in his lively affairs, he will not see any success," said the Holy Prophet. Without patience we won't be successful in our lives - the Prophet makes that very clear to us with this analogy.

At the end, if all else fails and you are searching for the most basic and practical way to be patient... count to ten. Count all ten chapters of this book and read them, it'll help you tremendously. That was a joke but seriously read the chapters, we think you'll enjoy it.

Three

Be Happy

EVERYONE WANTS TO BE HAPPY

Everyone wants to be happy. It is one of the most universal pursuits of life. We will come to realize that our happiness is so deeply connected to our relationship with God that without such a relationship, happiness is virtually impossible. And more specifically, in order for us to be happy we are in need of being in a state of appreciation and thankfulness to God. That thankfulness is directly linked to our contentment with God's blessings.

God is the Awarder of the Thankful – *Al-Shakour*. In order for us to be happy, we are going to need to beseech God and be thankful to Him for all that we have. One of the greater blessings we are thankful to God for is that of Ashura. Our scholars have said, "All that we have is from the blessing of Ashura." That day when Imam Hussain sacrificed everything for his Lord so that freedom, justice, and humanity never die.

THE GATEWAY TO HAPPINESS

"If Hussain had fought to quench his worldly desires...then I do not understand why his sister, wife, and children accompanied him. It stands to reason therefore, that he sacrificed purely for Islam."[7]

---

[7] Charles Dickens, Bentley's Miscellany, p. 61.

When Imam Hussain came forward in opposition to the rule of Yazid ibn Muawiya, it was a stance of principle. It was not only that Yazid occupied Imam Hussain's right in assuming the caliphate; his father Muawiya had usurped that very same right before, and yet Imam Hussain did not rise in revolt. Rather, it was because of Yazid's presence at the helm and his blatant deviation, along with the Umayyad machine that had developed, that Islam was at risk of being destroyed. It is for that reason Imam Hussain would rise – to protect Islam, even if it would mean his life. As one poet eloquently describes from the Imam's perspective, "If the religion of Muhammad will not remain intact except by my death, then O' swords take me." This is an individual who truly knew what balance was. He was one who saw test and trial, took them on and only achieved in the most excellent way. He was, in the simplest terms, the embodiment of happiness, living it in every second of his lifetime and giving it every second after his martyrdom.

Some may question how we can even talk about 'happiness' when it comes to Imam Hussain. His tragedy is such a sad, sorrowful, and heartbreaking story. All we can do in this regard, whenever his story is mentioned, is weep and cry. We dress in black and bury ourselves in sorrow for the undying tragedy that took place so many years ago. Why do we cry for Imam Hussain? Beyond the fact that his tragedy stands unique as the greatest witnessed by mankind. We cry for him because we realize how much he sacrificed for us and how far we actually are from his path. But we remind ourselves that by remembering Hussain, taking him into our hearts, and keeping him in our lives we can realize our purpose. We can realize our potential in life. We can become the best people we can possibly be. By holding on to the sacrifice, the principles, and the legacy of Imam Hussain we can realize happiness. He was selfless even with all the odds against him. He was generous even to those that stole everything from him. He was merciful to his friends, family, and even the barbarians that would kill his children. Hussain was the emanating mercy of God serving as a reminder to everyone who saw him or heard of him. He embodied every universal principle humanity lives by.

Imam Hussain reminds us that everything we have and everything we do is ultimately from God. "Lord, take from me until you are pleased," were his recurring words on the plains of Karbala. He was so strong in his faith because he knew that everything he had and everything that was, belonged to God. He appreciated that in every moment and was thankful. Yes, even during the tragedy he was thankful. And that is one of the keys to happiness – thankfulness. God tells us in the Holy Quran, "Surely We have shown him the way; he may be thankful or ungrateful."[8]

WE HAVE SO MANY BLESSINGS

Like the verse above says, we can be thankful or unthankful. It's for us to decide. Our response to the blessings of God is in our hands. We can see gratefulness in so many different settings. When a newborn is delivered in the hospital not only coming to life in its own physical state but bringing life to a household of a married couple – that little baby just made their family so much bigger. Take a walk outside in the beginning of autumn and watch the leaves on the trees change colors – red, orange, yellow – and fall to the ground making a painting of their own on God's earth. Pay close attention at the airport and watch as family members who haven't seen each other for years embrace each other and cry tears of joy. We all have experienced or at least witnessed some of these examples. When we take a step back to reflect we can see how amazing all of these simple things are, and we cannot help but be appreciative, grateful, and thankful to God for his infinite blessings.

Consider the technology that we have developed over the years and the strides we have made in

---

[8] The Holy Quran, 76:3.

communication, standard of living, and comfort. Can you remember the days when people held what were basically black bricks to their ears and called them cellphones? Do you remember what people used to do before the internet with regards to communication and networking? How many people have house phones nowadays, and if they have them how often do they use them? The applications, the programs, the games, all the technology is really fascinating when you think about it and compare them to the norms of our past. These are all blessings from God and consequently points of reflection for us.

"Surely We have shown him the way..."[9] God shows us by all the different blessings He has given us, and ultimately by the message He sent through our Holy Prophet Muhammad which was safeguarded by the zeal, commitment, and sacrifice of the Ahlulbayt. The guidance is there. It is up to us to heed to it. It is up to us to acknowledge and be thankful or alternatively turn our backs to the light that shines upon us every day. The choice is ours.

So why should we be thankful to God? Simply, it is in our nature to show gratitude to those who treat us with goodness. When someone gives us a gift, no matter how small or large, we know that it is proper etiquette to show gratitude. We smile, say 'thank

---

[9] Ibid.

you,' and make the effort to gift them with something in return. Are we only taught this through acquired practice, trained behavior, and social expectation? Our parents raised us well in this regard, however gratitude is really a natural response to the kindness of others.

But gratitude is not simply a learned response. Zeinab doesn't consciously smile ear to ear when her sister gifts her that perfume she's wanted for so long. Ali doesn't remind himself to be so truly happy when he realizes his wife saved up throughout the year to buy him the ultimate football season ticket passes, which he never considered buying himself because it was far too expensive. Mariam doesn't plan on jumping out of her chair and hugging her father crazy tight when he surprises her with a new car as a college graduation present. We naturally show gratitude when others show us kindness and treat us well. All of these examples are gifts of material things, but look deeper into the gifts and the circumstances surrounding them.

Zeinab isn't smiling simply because she got the perfume she wanted, she's smiling because her sister was listening when they had passed by the perfume stand several months prior and took note of what she liked. Ali has been wanting those season tickets but he is much happier because he has such a wonderful wife that cares about what makes him happy.

Mariam never complained about not having a car throughout college. She never mentioned it. The fact that her parents got her a new car, and one that she really liked, made her feel in that very moment that hard work, patience, and humbleness really does pay off. All of these examples fall within this theme of thanking those that treat us with goodness. This is also a theme known in Arabic as *shukr el-mun'im*, which is discussed as an intrinsic drive to worship God as He is the ultimate provider of good.

But let's discuss a little more on nurture. Sometimes we learn lessons of thankfulness in the least expected ways. On a usual Friday night Jawad went over his sister Mariam's house. He and his family were all sitting together in the family room talking while the TV played in the background. They had just finished eating a heavy Italian meal – namely Mariam's famous lasagna. Jawad tells her she should open a restaurant but she has enough on her plate with her full-time job, two beautiful kids, training young professionals with nonprofit organizations, amongst other things. As Jawad sat on the couch, trying to resist his food coma after that awfully delicious meal, he craved something sweet. His niece, Kawthar, was nearby. She was three years old at the time. Jawad asks her to grab him a piece of chocolate that was lying on the coffee table. "Okay uncle," grabbing the small chocolate delight and walking it back to her uncle. Jawad smiled, took the piece of candy and started eating. She stood there in her place looking at Jawad as he chewed on the candy. Realizing she was still there he asked, "Want some chocolate?" She shook her head and replied, "What do you say?" "Huh?" he replied. "You have to say thank you uncle!"

The three-year-old niece reminded Jawad about thankfulness. His sister and brother-in-law had raised her in such a way that thankfulness became engrained in her mechanisms of interaction, which included expectation of others as well. When we raise our children to appreciate others and to follow that appreciation with the simple words of 'thank you,' it helps reinforce the natural inclination we have toward gratitude. When we appreciate one another, we ultimately appreciate God. Because if we don't appreciate the blessings that God has given us through each other, we definitely don't appreciate Him.

HE GIVES US EVERYTHING

"And He gives you of all that you ask Him; and if you count Allah's favors you will not be able to number them; most surely man is very unjust, very ungrateful."[10] Indeed, God gives us all that we ask for. But

---

[10] The Holy Quran, 13:34.

some of us may question and say, "I've asked God for things and haven't gotten them... so how is this true?" Getting what we ask for is conditioned upon a number of things, one of them being gratefulness. Another condition is that God does not give us things that are not good for us. Sometimes we pray for things that are inherently harmful for us. If Ahmad prays to God to let him win the poker game he is planning to play tonight, does that sound like a prayer that God will answer? There is a problem in the prayer itself, a flaw in the perception of the one praying, not in the one receiving the prayer. God only plans the best for us. If something doesn't happen the way we wanted, rest assured that God has your best interest in mind and is protecting you so long as you place your trust in him. Gratefulness is key to that trust and protection. Still, even when we are ungrateful God continues to shower us with His blessings. It makes you think: if God treats me this well when I am ungrateful, how great would He treat me if I were thankful and devoted.

Have patience, because God knows what He is doing. Instead of asking God for specific things that you think are good or best for you, ask God to allow for the best to happen no matter what it is. While we are very far from knowing everything, God is omniscient. He knows all. The power, the might, the ability, the plan, is in His hands. So trust in Him and realize that the universe is much bigger than us to feel disappointed because we didn't get what we wanted. If we were to compare the things we didn't get to all that we have, the scales would tip drastically in favor of the latter. And all those blessings cannot be counted. Whether it's a graduate program that you were declined acceptance to, a job prospect that fell through, a marriage that was in the planning but didn't work out... no matter what the situation, know that God knows what is best for you. He knows us better than we know ourselves. Trust in Him. We came from Him, and we'll go back to Him.

The verse above is so powerful, "if you count Allah's favors you will not be able to number them..."[11] If we were to reflect on that, how could we be anything but infinitely grateful to God? Realize that when we read these verses from the Holy Quran, we are reading the unadulterated, unbothered, unchanged word of God. Some people ask for a sign. They say that they need God to show them the way and wish that God would just speak to them. God speaks to us every day – that is the miracle of the Holy Quran. All we need to do is open that book and hear what He has to say to us. God is speaking to us, but are we listening? "Therefore remember Me, I will remember you.

---

[11] Ibid.

And be thankful to Me, and do not be ungrateful to Me."[12]

REMEMBER HIM, HE WILL REMEMBER YOU

"And when your Lord proclaimed: If you give thanks I will give you more, but if you are thankless my punishment is dire."[13] Punishment is dire? That may make some of us feel uneasy. Well it should. Think about it: God created everything. Within the natural order of His creation He has embedded consequences to actions. If thankfulness brings happiness and success, it would naturally follow that thanklessness would bring misery and failure. Misery and failure lies in God's discontentment, and His discontentment brings forth punishment. This is a simple logical flow of actions and consequences.

Here's some more logic: before God created us, did we happen to do anything that made us deserving of existence? You might find the question to be absurd and ask, "How could we have done something to be deserving of existence before we even existed?" Exactly. Before anything was created, it did not have the ability to act and earn a status of entitlement. Thus, everything was brought into existence by the mercy of God – nothing else.

---

[12] The Holy Quran, 2:152.
[13] The Holy Quran, 14:7.

But be careful not to misuse that notion of mercy.

DON'T TAKE GOD FOR GRANTED

Some of us take a laid back approach when it comes to God and often say, "Don't worry God is merciful." We may try to convince ourselves to do things that are immoral, to indulge in vices, to disrespect ourselves with a lack of modesty and humility, all with the premise that "God is merciful." How many of us have heard the phrase, "It's just a small sin." The Holy Prophet is reported to have said, "Do not look at [how small] the sin is, but rather look at who it is that you sinned against."[14]

Our fourth Imam, Imam Al-Sajjad, fell ill on the journey to Karbala and could not fight alongside his brothers because of his illness – a divine wisdom which protected the imamate and the lineage of the Holy Prophet. This same Imam has a beautiful supplication known as *Dua Aba Hamza Athamali*. In one part of *Dua Aba Hamza*, the Imam describes the state of the believer speaking to God and grieving over his sins.

> *I am the one who did not revere You when I sinned in my seclusions, nor did I observe Your commands in public. I am the possessor of the great craftiness*

---

[14] Al-Tusi, *Al-Amali*, 528.

of bad intentions. I am the one who challenged his Master. I am the one who disobeyed the Commander of the skies... I am the one who when I was forewarned of the sin, I hastily raced to it. I am the one whom You awaited but I did not comprehend. You veiled my secrets but still I was not bashful, and I continued to commit sins belligerently insisting on it...

The first step in changing for the better is acknowledging the wrong that we have done. This is essential.

So, of course God is merciful. He is the most merciful. No one is more merciful than He. However, are we deserving of His mercy? After all the sin and vice we continue to indulge in, do we deserve his clemency and benevolence? If you had an employee who showed up late to work all the time, barely put any effort into his job, mistreated other employees at the office, was disrespectful, and did not even appreciate the opportunity given to him to be working in your firm, would you keep that employee around? Or would you fire him after the first few days of being a lousy employee? Most definitely the latter. The reality is God continues to shower us with His infinite mercy but it would be a grave mistake to take that for granted. Moreover, it would definitely not be in our favor to mistake that mercy for lack of consequence.

When God is giving us such a clear path, do we have any excuse? When we have someone like Imam Hussain give everything that he had for the sake of upholding truth and pleasing God, what excuse do we have not to fall in line and follow God's guidance? Imam Hussain gave himself, his family, his companions, everything he had for the sake of God. The Imam held his own six-month-old child, raising him on one arm to show the enemies across the battlefield how thirsty his baby was. He pled with them to give the child water. Instead of a cup of water they delivered an arrow to the neck of young Abdullah. His baby boy was killed in his hands. There was so much blood that came from this baby you would think it was the blood of a man. Looking at his lifeless son and then to the heavens, the Imam said, "This is all for you my Lord..." The patience, the balance, the sacrifice – he gave it all for God. God gives us the blessing of Imam Hussain so that we know what thankfulness is. The path of guidance is not unclear, it's not ambiguous, we know what we need to do – we just need to do it.

In *Surat Al-Kahf* (The Cave) of the Holy Quran, God tells us the story of two friends. One of the friends was rich and the other was poor. The rich friend owned vast lush orchards where he grew a variety of delicious fruit. He was doing very well for himself. His business was thriving, he was high up in the social ladder, he had everything he wanted – life was good. The poor friend advises his rich friend to show thanks to God and be grateful. He explains that everything is from God and nothing we have is independent from His blessing; we should show thanks to God so that He is pleased with us and add to the favor He has already bestowed upon us. The rich friend wasn't buying it. The more money he had, the more arrogant and ungrateful he became. He replied that he had everything going for him and he was in no need to thank God. After some days passed, the rich friend approaches his orchards for a regular management visit and found an unpleasant surprise. His moneymaking days were over. The orchards were completely flooded and the crops were destroyed. "If I had thanked God and did not disbelieve, this would not have happened," He regretfully said.

HAPPINESS LIES AT A MOTHER'S FEET

If we want to be thankful to God, we need to be thankful to our mothers. Our mothers did for us what no one could do. Regarding the right of the mother, Imam Sajjad said,

> The right of your mother is that you know that she carried you where no one carries anyone, she gave to you of the fruit of her heart that which no one

gives to anyone, and she protected you with all her organs. She did not care if she went hungry as long as you ate, if she was thirsty as long as you drank, if she was unclothed as long as you were clothed, if she was in the sun as long as you were in the shade. She gave up sleep for your sake, she protected you from heat and cold, all in order that you might belong to her... You will not be able to show her gratitude, without God's help.[15]

If we take the time to acknowledge and appreciate our mothers for their grace and blessing over us we would understand why the Holy Prophet said, "Heaven is at the feet of the mothers." He didn't say that Heaven is in her arms or in her midst, he said that it lies at her very feet. If we want God's pleasure, if we want to be within the eternal grace and mercy of God, we should look no further than being the best sons and daughters to our mothers. It is simple. Be a great son. Be a great daughter. Be there for your mother whenever she needs you, because you owe that to her at the very least. We owe it to our mothers and our fathers – we'll get to our fathers in a minute – to be kind to them, respect them, heed their advice and requests, and most of all be there for them even when they don't ask us to.

---

[15] Imam Ali Al-Sajjad, Treatise on Rights, Right #22.

Another thing. Don't talk back to your mother. Don't break your mother's heart with your sharp tone. Imam Ali tells us, "Do not use the sharpness of your tongue on the mother who taught you how to speak." Imagine how painful it is to see your child, the one you brought into this world, speak to you in a demeaning way. How hurt would you be if your 'pride and joy' rolled their eyes at you and walked away dismissively? We should show nothing but love, respect, and honor to our mothers and fathers. Love is not a feeling. Respect is not a sentiment. Honor is not simply symbolic. These things are realized through actions and behavior. Our state of mind manifests through our conduct. If we can't patiently listen to our parents' perspectives then we are showing them we don't value their thoughts and experience. What you show is usually indicative of what's inside. "I don't mean it like that," doesn't always fly. "You know I love you," can only go so far. The way we are with our loved ones and the way we see the world is entirely up to us. We choose to be respectful, loving, thankful, and ultimately happy.

Someone came up to the Holy Prophet asking for the Prophet's blessing and a word of advice. The Prophet gave him two words, "Your mother." Take care of your mother he emphasized. The man asked the Prophet again for further advice, as in what else he thinks is important. The Prophet replied again,

"Your mother." The man asked a third time. To that the Prophet said, "Your mother and your father." Don't forget about your father. Imam Sajjad says,

> The right of your father is that you know that he is your root. Without him, you would not be. Whenever you see anything in yourself which pleases you, know that your father is the root of its blessing upon you.[16]

THE GREATNESS OF CONTENTMENT

Thankfulness is key to our happiness. So is contentment. Though the two go hand in hand we can't neglect the importance of knowing what it means to be content. If we focus our hearts and minds on contentment we can realize true happiness. So what is contentment? Contentment is finding that inner peace with whatever situation you are in.

Some people never find happiness. That is often because they are not content with their lives. They are not content with the blessings they have. In fact, they may look at some blessings as burdens or even take what good they have for granted. Take Ziyad for example. Ziyad is 34 years old. After graduating with a master's degree in business administration, he landed a corporate job and gradually climbed the

---

[16] Imam Ali Al-Sajjad, Treatise on Rights. Right #23.

corporate ladder. Now he's one of the top executives - and the youngest - at his company. He is married to his best friend – Layla – a critical care nurse who loves to help people. They live in a quiet New Jersey suburb with their two beautiful children, Ali and Zahra, who are eight and six. Ziyad should be perfectly happy, right? Sadly, he's not. Though he has a loyal wife, beautiful healthy children, and a great career, he constantly feels like something is missing. A bigger house? They just moved to a new 3000 square foot home. A newer car? He drives a brand new 2015 Cadillac CTS. Vacation perhaps? They just got back from an all-inclusive resort trip to the Caribbean. So what's missing? Nothing is missing, he just doesn't realize how much he has.

You see it's not what we have, but how we choose to have it. Ziyad is not missing anything. The emptiness he feels is his own lack of contentment, which is his fault alone. A man can have all the money in the world and still be poor. Unfortunately, we often do not realize how much we have until we lose it. And even when we lose it we become bitter instead of humbled, harsh instead of kind, and ungrateful for the time we had instead of thankful. Here's a simple statistic that you might have heard: over 2 billion people around the world live on less than $2 per day. That is a little over $700 per year. Can you imagine that?

Do we realize the blessings that we have? Do we realize that our contentment, our happiness, lies within us? We choose to be content. We choose to be happy. Be mindful that being content doesn't mean that we are not ambitious. Being content means that we are striving for greatness but accept the cards we are dealt; working with what we have to the best of our ability. Being content means that we make opportunities out of perceived failures and keep moving forward. We are not bogged down with what has passed us and instead work towards what we can attain. We see the blessing we live in, appreciate our past experiences, and strive for better in the future. Being content means that we dream. Yes, we dream sky high. But we are grounded. We smile where we stand.

The words of Imam Ali sum it up perfectly.

> *Blessed is the man who always kept the life after death in his view, who worked towards the Day of Judgment, who led a contented life, and who was happy with God [and what He has given him].*

Keep your eye on the prize. Don't lose sight of things. Remember that balance is instrumental to our success, to our happiness. If we lose sight of our purpose, of our higher calling, then we will lose track of ourselves. We won't find the goodness that lies in everything. We will be negative and bitter.

"If you cannot get the things that you want, then be content with what you have." Don't be a person who complains about all the things they don't have. How do we expect to be happy in life when all we look at is what we don't have. When was the last time you thought about all the things you do have? Take this as an exercise. Pull out a sheet of paper and a pen, or your smart phone if you're not old-fashioned. Jot down your main body parts. From each body part put down all the things you do with that body part or component (your mind and soul included). Develop the list and add to it day by day. Look back to the list from time to time and think to yourself, 'what would I do without this body part?' Think about it. Reflect. Appreciate the bounties of the blessings you have and be content.

Is your cup half full or half empty? The classic question that is indicative of our perspective and mindset. People that answer half full are positive, content, happy people. Be positive. Be content. Be happy.

Four

Be Humble

PUT YOUR BLAME FINGER DOWN

God is just. He is the Just. Any form of justice that we know of is essentially from God. So is it that God adheres to a system whereby we can evaluate God's 'actions' as meeting the standards of justice? In this suggestion can we say that what God did here is 'just' and what he did there was 'unjust'? Or is it that God Himself is the standard by which we apply ourselves rather than applying Him to a standard we have manufactured? In fact, everything that exists flows from God's justice and from Him we know what is just and what is not. This is an essential philosophical distinction that is extremely relevant to our worldview, our perspective of God, and our role in it all.

On a more practical level, we decipher this lesson of justice to better meet the challenges that come our way. How do we deal with the tests and trials we face? When a problem or mishap takes place, when is it my responsibility or my fault even? When is it someone else's fault? And even when it is the fault or responsibility of others, what is my role in dealing with the situation to what would be my best interest?

On the eve of Ashura, Imam Hussain gathered all of his companions. The loyal champions rushed to surround their leader, eager to hear the little he had to say in those somber hours in what would be their last night together. It was as if that was the darkest night anyone there had ever seen and still it shined brilliantly with their beaming faces of hope. Imam Hussain did not need to speak of the events that would unfold the next day; they all knew their ending fate. Still, they only smiled to the thought of it. He told his faithful companions that they were free to leave in the night and that the enemies only thirsted for *his* blood. He urged them to take the cover of the dark night and ride on their horses to faraway lands and spare their lives. He assured them that he would not *blame* them and they were free to go on their way. The band of companions did not move an inch. Their feet only dug deeper in the sand of Karbala. One of the companions stepped forward to the Imam and said unwaveringly, "Hussain, we will never leave you." And then another said earnestly wishing he could say more, "For you a thousand times over." *A thousand times over.* They echoed those words to their very last breath.

Beyond the themes of sacrifice, courage, and loyalty that echoed throughout the story of Karbala we want to shed some light on what Imam Hussain mentioned on the eve of Ashura. He said he would not *blame* his companions for leaving. He claimed all responsibility and wanted to spare his closest friends, his brothers, of any harm or fault. There was no blame when it came to Imam Hussain. But why? Wouldn't you expect your closest friends to be there when you needed them most? Why wouldn't Imam Hussain blame them if they actually did leave him? Wouldn't they be deserving of blame if they did leave? Imam Hussain didn't look at it that way. He looked at things with regard to his responsibility and contribution to any given situation. Yes, it may have reflected badly on the companions if they left but all in all it was his battle not theirs. Their loyalty would show their commitment and virtue; however, his own commitment would not rely on theirs. Thus, he would reassure them that he would not blame them for taking their leave. This actually went to crystalize the Imam's own commitment, love, and faithfulness to his family, friends, and principles. To the very end he only wanted the best for his loved ones, even when he faced the worst of odds and the weight of the world was on his shoulders.

We definitely do not face the challenges they faced, but do we implement their steadfastness and commitment? If not entirely, at least partly? If not, we can definitely commit ourselves to reassessing the way we do things and see how we can be inspired towards betterment by their examples – the companions in their commitment and Imam Hussain in his compassion.

Expectations and Blame

We go about our lives with expectations. It's natural. We all have expectations of each other and ourselves. Expectations lead to assumptions of responsibility and assumptions of responsibility lead to blame. Often our expectations of others seem to overshadow what we expect of ourselves and thus our blame usually extends to others before ourselves in the same way.

Adam is taking Near Eastern History as part of his general education courses at his university. The course has a tasking written final that makes up 60% of the total grade in the class. He knows that he needs to spend a few hours each day in the week prior to the exam to adequately prepare for it. He knows this because the professor clearly stated this throughout the semester on a number of occasions. On top of that, several upperclassmen told Adam that he should take it seriously. Adam has done great in classes throughout high school and community college without needing to study much. So, he brushes off the advice, shrugs and plays video games for the majority of his time building up to the exam. He decides to study just a couple hours before the big day, rely on his wits and the ideas he's 'grasped' over the course of the semester. Adam fails the exam. Because he failed the exam, Adam failed the course. Now he has to retake the course. You would expect that Adam would blame no one but himself right? Wrong. Adam chooses to blame his professor for being 'too strict' and the course as 'dumb.' He even tells some of his friends that he failed because the professor was 'racist against Arabs.' Funny how the professor was of Arab descent himself.

You can see how ridiculous Adam may sound in retrospect. Adam saw that as well, much later on though. Still, we all have these sorts of tendencies. When we can't seem to find our keys, it's *'who moved my keys?'* When its seems that we misplaced our wallet, it's *'someone stole my wallet!'* Remember in elementary school, *'who took my notebook?'* or *'someone stole my pencil!'* and the classic *'my dog ate my homework.'* The last one is often a darn outright lie because most don't even have a dog to begin with. But you see this constant theme of shifting blame and attributing fault to people other than ourselves, even when we don't know who they are. Adam had no one to blame but himself. We usually are the ones who have moved our keys or wallets, dropped our pencils, forgot our notebooks at home, or didn't do our homework at all.

SO WHO CAN I BLAME?

But even in situations where others may be to blame, is that the best option for us? It is important for us to realize that as much as we would like to think otherwise, we don't have control over other people's actions. Yes, we can influence, suggest, insinuate, guide, or even deceive, but ultimately each individual has his or her own decision. We have control over ourselves – nothing more and nothing less. You control how you behave, what you do, what you believe, how you engage and even how you perceive things. And because of that, you dictate your own happiness. The more we realize how central this is to our success and happiness the more successful we will be and the happier we will become. This essentially means that in order for us to be successful in anything we do, we need to take responsibility in the problems we face and ask ourselves the essential question, "How did I contribute to this and how can I make a change?"

There is an inherent weakness that lies in shifting blame to others. When we don't want to accept responsibility and navigate the possibilities of our contribution to the given situations we are in, we are giving up our own power that allows us to fix problems. In shifting blame we only exacerbate issues instead of resolving them. Remember, we can't control the actions and contributions of others. We control ourselves. So the greatest utility would come simply from reflecting on how *we* have contributed, what *we* can do differently, and what *we* need to work on. This will allow us to take control of our problems, address them effectively and move forward positively.

So, you lost your wallet, you failed your exam, you got in a car accident, you lost your job... whatever the case may be, extreme or not extreme, what do you do in that situation? Do you start blaming people? Consider the following story: Mousa and Jamal are driving to their favorite burger joint. About a mile before reaching the burger joint, Mousa approaches a traffic light turning yellow. He slows down to come to a stop. The driver behind him doesn't make the same decision and *Bam*! Mousa and Jamal get out of the car to see the damage made to the rear end of their car. The other driver gets out of his car and yells out, "Why did you stop?!" Mousa calmly replies, "Bro, it was a red light." "You shouldn't have stopped, I was still going!" Mousa and Jamal look at each other speechless. "It was a red light and you wanted us to keep going? You hit us after we stopped at a red light. How are you blaming us for that?" Jamal said to the nervous rear-ender. "Bro, I'm not blaming you but you shouldn't have stopped you had time to keep going," he unabashedly replied. Mousa and Jamal were nice but they didn't feel too bad when the police showed up and handed the other guy a hefty ticket.

The sad thing is that we do this kind of stuff all the time. With our siblings, our colleagues, our parents, and others, we think about how they affected the situation before anything else. Like we said earlier, the first question that we really need to ask ourselves is, "How did I contribute to the problem or situation at hand?"

Looking For Others' Flaws

There is a common theme here and throughout the whole book. It's about our perspective. Our attitude. The way we *choose* to see things and deal with them. Part of the problem of blaming others is the deep negativity that lies in it. When we get in the habit of blaming others we spew out negativity. There's nothing great about being negative. It is notably unhelpful, pessimistic, and unconstructive. The same negativity used in the blame game is seen with some of us who have taken it upon ourselves to pinpoint all the flaws in those around us. Some have taken the task so seriously it's like a full-time job. We can't go a day without pointing fingers at others and seeing what's wrong with *them*.

There's a concept called *weatherproofing* that some self-development teachers use in this regard. When winter approaches we go out of our way to make sure that our houses are well prepared for the cold season. We check our windows, doors, and basement foundation for cracks and proper sealing. We do this to make sure no cold air is seeping through which inevitably will increase our heat bill and add discomfort to an already challenging season. So, to properly weatherproof we are keen to searching for the smallest areas that need to be sealed, fixed, or replaced. We're *looking* for the defects, the flaws, the deficiencies no matter how small they may be. Though weatherproofing is great to use for your house, car, and business, it is not the same when using it on your family, friends, and colleagues.

For some reason, we like to criticize one another. We criticize almost everyone we know. The people we love, those we work with, and even strangers. We're sure that you, the reader, have been criticized plenty. We all have. At the same time, you've probably done your own fair share of criticizing others. We all have. When we are criticized by our friends or family it's not the most pleasant experience. At the least, it doesn't make us *feel* good. When your sister is criticizing the way you dress, even if it is she intends it as constructive criticism, you're not particularly gleaming with joy. Why? She means well. She's my sister. I know she has my best interest in mind. Nonetheless, we are sensitive to our own shortcomings, weaknesses, and imperfections. So, the *way* we come across in giving each other constructive criticism is key. No matter how constructive the intention, if it sounds like plain old criticism, the receiving end won't buy it.

Take the example of Zeinab and Susan. Zeinab, 18, and Susan, 15, are sisters. Zeinab's wardrobe is more conservative and she tends to err on the side of caution when it comes to what she wears. Caution? So basically she doesn't wear tight or suggestive clothes. Her outfits are usually long and loose. No skinny jeans for Zeinab. Susan on the other hand likes to experiment a bit more with her outfits. She thinks that if you have a nice body you should show it off. "The tigher the better," she says. Oh, and she *loves* colors! "The brighter the better," she adds. At the same time, she tries to incorporate the latest fashions into her outfits. She likes to think that her outfits express her beauty and creativity. In a nutshell, modesty is a top priority for Zeinab when it comes how she dresses, but it's secondary on Susan's checklist of colors, latest fashion, and what she considers to be *cute*.

Zeinab cares about her younger sister. She wants Susan to make smarter choices. On a Friday evening, Zeinab and Susan are getting ready to go to the movies with their cousins and some friends. Zeinab is ready in about 20 minutes, while Susan has been in her room getting ready for almost an hour. After waiting for an hour, Zeinab comes into Susan's room to hurry her along. She opens the door and finds Susan posing in front of her mirror. Wearing black skinny jeans and a shirt that barely comes down past the buckle of her pants, Susan looks at Zeinab through the mirror and says, "Don't I look so cute in this?" Zeinab puts her hands on her waist and waits for her thoughts to gather on how to reply to her sister's trivial question.

So how does Zeinab approach this recurring issue with her sister? Look at the difference between these two statements: "Seriously Susan? What you're wearing is ridiculous. Change your clothes before you embarrass us," and "Susan you look really cute. I'm not sure if that's the best thing for you to wear outside the house though. You really don't want to send the wrong message to people." Remember, you can't control the actions of others. You can influence, suggest, and guide, but you can't make decisions for them. How receptive will Susan be to the first statement? Yes, it is her older sister and if she wants she could escalate this to her parents and make it a bigger problem – a temporary deterrent for Susan. But, that won't help Susan in making better choices for herself. The second response by Zeinab is much more appealing to a teenager struggling with expression and individuality without sacrificing principles and modesty.

Even when we are in the right to criticize, point out flaws, or even reprimand, there is a way to go about it. But in general, having the priority to look for others' flaws is deeply wrong and misguided. To shift this culture of attitude and behavior, we need to start with ourselves. If we don't like to get criticized, then we need stop criticizing other people. Again, what can you control other than your own actions? By you stopping a certain action or habit you indirectly, or maybe even directly, influence others to do the same.

Did You See Where This Guy Was?

"If you don't have anything nice to say, don't say anything at all." Of the many important lessons that our parents and teachers taught us when we were younger, this one reigns in this discussion. So simple and so true. God says in the Holy Quran, "O you who have faith! Avoid much suspicion; indeed some suspicions are sins."[17] What does it mean to be *suspicious*? Let's say you're driving down Michigan Avenue. It's a beautiful day. Your windows are down, no need for AC. The forecast is 76°F, clear skies, and a high chance of Barbeque. As you're cruising on this glorious day you see your friend walking. Before you get a chance to pull over and say *Salaam*, you see him walk into the entrance of a building. It's not just any

---

[17] The Holy Quran, 49:12.

old building – it's the underground club. Well, rumor has it that there is an underground club in the building, but it really is an office building. Nonetheless, you're shocked. Disappointed. Appalled even. 'How could he go into a place like that?' You think to yourself. 'I thought I knew him. I thought he was religious.' Again, you're not completely sure that he went to that infamous club. You didn't see him enter the door of a club and there are other offices and apartments in that building. Couldn't he be doing something else? Nah. You stick to the club-scene story and remain appalled. That is the kind of suspicion we're talking about. Mind you, it doesn't have to be something drastic like a club, bar, or something like that. It could be doubting someone's intentions in a conversation, or thinking someone has bad motives in the way they acted in a specific situation.

The Quran clearly tells us to avoid such suspicion and that suspicions are sins. Imam Ali tells us that when we see our believing brothers or sisters in a suspicious situation we should give them seventy excuses before we jump to a negative conclusion. *Seventy* excuses. Do we even try to give our family and friends one or two excuses, let alone seventy? The friend that you see supposedly walking into a suspicious place could be visiting an office in that building. Maybe you're eyes deceived you as you were driving and he actually walked into the entrance of the building next door instead. Before we jump to any nasty or negative conclusions we need to give each other the benefit of the doubt. In fact, we need to give each other seventy excuses if we want to follow the advice of our Imams.

Unfortunately, we sometimes fail to follow that advice. We even go off to talk about the things that we have seen, or things we think we have seen. Rumors spread and people's reputations are tarnished. It's sad to see that we can ruin people's lives simply by saying ill things about them. Sometimes words can be sharper than a knife and more lethal than a gun. You can kill someone with your words, maybe not their body but their name and even their spirit. That is why there is so much emphasis from the Holy Quran and the Ahlulbayt on how we interact with others, what we say to each other and about one another. "People are safe from the believer's tongue," Imam Ja'far Al-Sadiq said. Are people safe from our tongues? If they're not safe from us, we could very well be eating their dead flesh when we backbite them as the Quran tells us. The verse we previously mentioned continues and says, "Will any of you love to eat the flesh of his dead brother? You would hate it. Be wary of God; indeed God is all-clement, all-merciful."[18]

Do we realize the impact of backbiting? Do we realize what we are doing when we are pinpointing the flaws and defects of others and then speaking about them to others. By the way, backbiting here is not spreading false rumors about a person. Backbiting actually refers to spreading true defects, sins, or flaws a person has. So God is telling us that speaking of someone's *actual* defect, sin, or flaw is like eating the flesh of your dead brother. Yes. You don't need to be lying or spreading a false rumor for your words to carry such cruel weight. When we're *chillin'* with our friends and just hanging out, we need to be very careful of the things we say. Remember what we were taught when we were kids, "If you don't have anything nice to say, don't say anything at all."

And remember that if you know something bad about someone and you share it, you're really hurting yourself. Some narrations say that when we backbite a believer the angels that record our deeds make an interesting swap between us. They take all of our good deeds and record it as credit for the person we just spoke ill of, and here's the grand slam; they take all of their bad deeds and record them in our book of debts, sins, and misfortune. How's that

---

[18] The Holy Quran, 49:12.

for a transaction? So the next time we think about backbiting someone let's ask ourselves, is it worth it?

FOCUS ON YOU

Imam Ali gives us a deep perspective on the issue of how we should look at other people's sins and our own. He says, "Do not be quick in exposing other people's sins, for God may have forgiven them. And do not feel yourself safe, even for a small sin, because you may be punished for it..." So don't worry about other people's sins and how 'bad' they are. We need only to worry about ourselves. If we reflect we can see the mountains of flaws, shortcomings, and sins we have accumulated over the years. We are in no position to be exposing others, prying into other people's business and worrying ourselves with who did what, when, and where. Let's not waste our time and damn ourselves at the same time. We have to take responsibility over our own lives. If you can help others, great! But if you can't then leave them be, don't talk about them, and focus on yourself.

"Whoever acts righteously, it is for his own soul, and whoever does evil, it is to its own detriment, then you will be brought back to your Lord."[19] When we act righteously, when we are kind, when we do

---

[19] The Holy Quran, 45:15.

something good, we are in essence doing it for ourselves. It benefits us in this life and the next. Mahmoud gives charity to a beggar on the street. When Mahmoud helps the poor guy, God increases Mahmoud's sustenance and will reward him in the afterlife as well. Of course the beggar is benefiting from Mahmoud's spare change, but that change that Mahmoud is sparing goes to benefit Mahmoud even more. In the same way, if Mahmoud were to mistreat that beggar, Mahmoud would suffer from that wrongdoing in this life and the next. Basically, what you do affects you in ways that you may not even see. If you do good things, you'll enjoy good consequences. If you do bad things, you'll suffer bad consequences. Simple.

It's also important to think about the acts that involve no one but ourselves – meaning our acts of worship directly to God. Take for example, our prayers. Some people mistakenly believe that because God commands us to pray, we are evidently praying for Him. He commands us to pray so we pray. Are we really praying for God? Meaning, does God need our prayers and because He needs them He has commanded us to pray? And because we are subservient to Him we obey and pray? This is one big fallacy. God does not need our prayers. In His essence and one of the most fundamental attributes of God is His lack of need – His self-sufficient independence. We pray because *we need* our prayers. We pray because it is the best thing for us to do. In fact, any commandment given to us by God – to do or don't – is in our best interest. So basically, we are praying *to* God but *for* ourselves.

BE HUMBLE

In focusing on ourselves, we need to realize the great importance of humility. Be humble. Imam Hassan teaches us volumes in humbleness and humility. One day he came across a few children sitting down on the ground in a nearby neighborhood. As the Imam approached, the children exchanged *Salaams* with the Imam. The children asked him to join them and eat with them. All they had was a hard loaf of bread. The Imam smiled. When they finished eating, the Imam gathered the children and gave them new clothes, money, and other gifts. When some of the Imam's family and companions asked about the children he told them of the hospitality he received from the children. He said that no matter what he has given them it is still not as much as what they gave him. Puzzled they waited for an explanation from their Imam. He explained that he has given them and still has more to give, but the children offered him everything they had even though it was only a piece of bread.

Humbleness is key to our own success and happiness. It is easier said than done. But if we remind ourselves of how small we are in comparison to the grandeur of God and His universe we can keep ourselves in check. This is in no way to demean ourselves or belittle our potential. Not at all. Even the great prophets continued to remind themselves of their dependence on God and how insignificant they were without their Lord. Our greatness as individuals comes with knowing our potential through God and being grounded in the reality that nothing can be achieved without His grace and blessing.

"The servants of the All-beneficent are those who walk humbly on the earth, and when the ignorant address them, say, 'Peace!'"[20] Being 'religious' is not only about our prayers and fasting, it's about how we conduct ourselves in private and in public. Walk humbly. Lower your graze. Be proud of who you are but be grounded in that as well, because you are a creation of God and a follower of His Truth. You can do amazing things in this life, so long as you remember where your grace and blessings come from – so long as you don't lose sight of that Truth. It is when we lose sight of God's Truth that we become arrogant, thankless, and oppressive. Imam Ali said,

---

[20] The Holy Quran, 25:63.

I wonder at the arrogant man who was just a drop of semen the other day, and will turn into a rotting corpse tomorrow. I wonder at the man who doubts God although he sees His creations. I wonder at him who has forgotten death although he sees people dying. I wonder at him who denies the second life although he has seen the first life. I wonder at him who inhabits this transient abode but ignores the everlasting abode. I wonder at one who is careful in selecting his food for fear of illness, but is not careful in his actions for fear of hellfire.[21]

We need to look ourselves in the mirror and remind ourselves of our origins, where we came from, where everything came from. It is great to be confident, but we can't let our confidence lead us to arrogant pride. Arrogance helps no one. It is a façade that only deepens a person in illusion and makes it harder to wake up and see life for what it is – an opportunity. We have the opportunity to be great and be humble – a balance that only few realize and achieve. "The sin that displeases you is better in the view of God than the virtue which makes you proud."[22] Think about that. God would rather see you sin and feel guilt and regret than see you do something good that will turn you arrogant. Imagine if you could strike the balance in doing good and remaining

---

[21] Al-Sabzawari, *Jami' Al-Akhbar*, 360.
[22] Imam Ali, *The Peak of Eloquence*, Saying 46.

humble, refraining from wrongdoing, but when you fall you regret and repent. Imagine that. We can do it. We just need to keep ourselves in check. Remind ourselves of what is important and surround ourselves in environments that are positive, free of backbiting and negative criticism, and nurturing to our intellectual and spiritual growth.

This life is a journey. What are we going to do on the way? Because, quite simply, what we do on the way will be the reality that we live when we arrive at our new destination.

Five

Be Kind

The Kindness of God

God is *Al-Wadood* – the Loving. When we look around us we see that God's love encompasses us all.

> *Say [that God declares,] 'O My servants who have committed excesses against their own souls, do not despair of the mercy of God. Indeed God will forgive all sins. Indeed, He is the All-forgiving, the All-merciful.*[23]

No matter what situation you're in, no matter how hopeless you may feel – do not despair in God, because His mercy is ever-encompassing. That is how much He loves us, that no matter what He keeps His doors open for us. His door is always open, we simply choose not to enter.

We mentioned in a previous chapter some of the words of Imam Ali Al-Sajjad written in Dua Aba Hamza Athamali. Reflect on some more words from the Imam from the very same supplication. He says,

> *O' Master! I am the young one whom You raised. I am the ignorant whom You educated. I am the misled whom You guided. I am the humiliated one whom You elevated. I am the frightened one whom You safeguarded, the hungry one whom You fed, the thirsty whose thirst You quenched, the naked*

---
[23] The Holy Quran, 39:53.

whom You dressed, the poor whom You made wealthy, the weak whom You strengthened, the insignificant whom You honored, the sick whom You cured, the beggar whom You provided charity to, the sinner whose secret You have protected, and the wrong doer whom You aided. I am the little (creature) You made more significant, and the oppressed whom You made victorious...

Through the gift of parents, community, and God's unequivocal grace, we were brought up to be the people we are today. He provided us opportunities to learn and become educated. From our first day in kindergarten where we couldn't let go of Mama or Baba's hand to our graduation from college – He guided us through it all. Even when we strayed away from Him, He protected us and moved us forward. He never stopped blessing us nor will His blessings ever stop showering on us. When we were misguided, it was He who brought us back to see the light. There wasn't a time when we guided ourselves. We can't take the credit for our success independently – He was always there. God honored and elevated us when we would otherwise be humiliated. Even in the smallest things, He would guard us from people's mockery and humiliation. And whenever we did fall to be embarrassed or humiliated before people it was only to humble us or make us stronger.

Do you remember being scared as a child? Frightened by the dark or being alone? Do you remember maybe walking or driving in a neighborhood that just didn't feel right? What saved you and ended your fears? Your parents or a friend maybe, or maybe your own courage to carry on. Where did that courage come from? Who graced us with our parents, our friends, our bravery? None other than He. The food we eat, the water we drink, the clothes we wear – all sustenance and blessings of God. The fact that we can order a sandwich from our favorite sub-shop, go out to lunch with friends, have dinner on the table serving our favorite home-cooked meals with a side of Mama's love – all of these He provides.

We've all experienced some form of sickness, even as minor as the common cold. He brings us back to our feet to be healthy again and again. "Two blessings that people take for granted: health and security," Imam Ali said. The number of youth that suddenly fall ill or pass away unexpectedly should remind us of how fragile we are. It should ground us to realize how much we are in need of Him. Do you remember the times when you would look into your pockets and find money you didn't put there? Do you remember your first job? How excited you were to be finally working and making your own money? Do you remember your first promotion and how proud your family was of you? Or the time when your bank account only had a few dollars and that raised to a few hundred and then a few thousand? Your hard work does pay off, but the one that eases the way is no one but Him.

The only time we can really feel true strength is when we call His name. It is more innate that we think. In our heart of hearts we know that He is the only strength, the only source, and the only end for our hopes, dreams and aspirations. At the same time, He guarded us and protected our secrets even when we sinned against Him. Time and time again. We wronged Him. We dishonored ourselves and our name before Him. Still, he concealed our flaws and did not expose us in front of others. Some of us may grow discomforted by these thoughts, because it may seem negative and not 'forward-looking'. True, we are looking to the past. But we look to the past so that we may learn from our mistakes and ground ourselves with humility. If we forget our past, we will only repeat our mistakes once again. Repentance would only be an utterance of 'astaghfurallah' – nothing more. So learn from your past and move forward to acknowledge the greatness you can achieve.

God gives us the ability to reach our potential of excellence, to strive for the stars and achieve our greatness. God only wants great things for us – that could be why He gives us so many chances. Do not ever think you are insignificant – you're not. "You think you're insignificant while within you lies the greater universe," Imam Ali tells us. Our potential is endless, so long as we hold on to the Everlasting. And even when we are seemingly beaten, oppressed, and all the odds are against us – he makes us victorious. This is manifested in the person of Imam Hussain. A man who stood on the 10th Day witnessing the heart wrenching massacre of his brothers, sons, and companions before giving his own life and said, "This is all for You. Take until You are pleased, my Lord." This is what Karbala was about – being fully dissolved in Him. *This is all for You.*

NICE GUYS DON'T FINISH LAST

There's a saying that some people have – "Nice guys finish last." Though in some aspects it may not be entirely false within competitive cutthroat circles of business, it is not a solid rule in most aspects of life. Believe it or not, being nice has a great deal of benefits. Through kindness you gain people's trust. People feel safe around you. That trust can be the defining difference in a long-term business relationship. It can be what differentiates you from so many others. Even beyond what it may do for your business relationships and career, it makes you a more attractive person to befriend, love, and even care for. Your personal relationships will be tremendously enhanced by being nicer, kinder, or simply politer.

Try something different for a change. When you do something kind or nice, keep it to yourself. Do something nice for someone else and make sure not to tell anyone about it. We like people to know about the good things that we do. There's nothing wrong with that. It is natural for us to want others to think fondly of us. Of course, we should not be doing good things for that purpose but to acknowledge it and enjoy it as a natural consequence is not a problem. It's when our actions are driven by the desire to be acknowledged, praised or admired that will steer us in the wrong direction. So, make a donation to a poor family, an orphan charity, your local mosque, or any other charity, but – and here's the key – don't tell any about your donation. Make your donation anonymous. Yes, anonymous. What about my tax return? Your taxes will be fine. Just try this and see how it will benefit you. When you can look up and pray to God knowing that there are secrets between you and Him that extend beyond your sins, it is a tremendous feeling. Imagine you can confide in God with things other than your wrongdoing. You can pray to God that He accepts the good deeds you've done in secret, showing that you've done them only to please Him and no one else. That is powerful. Trust us. Try it.

Since we're on being nice and acting kindly, try practicing 'random' acts of kindness. Do kind things that are out of your norm. Beyond the typical donation at your mosque, be creative. Even if it is something as simple as helping your neighbor with the yard work, or donating your professional time to a local organization, or playing soccer with the neighborhood kids – whatever it may be. Be kind. And be kind in different ways. Mix it up for yourself. You'll see that the more kind you are in different ways, the greater peace you'll have for yourself. That kindness bringing you inner peace will spread to your friends and family. A new calm will surround you and your loved ones will feel it, and they will love you for it.

But isn't it hard to be kind all the time? Don't people tick you off sometimes? At times people can be so wrong and you just need to tell people off, right? Well, you can take that route. You may be even justified to do so. But how effective will that be? Yasser and his wife, Nadia, get in a fight. They're arguing over how he was not 'involved' enough at the discussion at Nadia's parents' house. "You never show you're interested!" She accuses. "Are you serious? What did I do?" Yasser responds. "Exactly. Nothing. Nothing at all. You don't say anything. You make it seem like you don't care about my parents and what they talk about," Nadia claims with frustration. "But I really don't care about what they talk about. I'm not going to be a phony about it," Yasser says earnestly. Offended Nadia sharply replies, "They know that! But you can at least be courteous and respectful instead of being such a jerk Yasser!"

Now, Nadia is right. Yasser should not be such a jerk. But, Nadia's hot temper is unlikely to move Yasser away from his cold demeanor. He will respond to her in the same way he responded to her parents – uninterested and brutally honest. Sometimes, we need to be kind in seeing what is meaningful from the other person's perspective and speak to them from that angle. We would especially employ this kind of approach when we find it really important to get across to someone.

CARE BECAUSE GOD DOES

It's sad at times that the people we care for the most, are the people we go out of our way for the least. Maybe we take each other for granted. Or maybe we think that the closest people to us already know how we feel or think about them. You may be thinking: Why would I need to tell my wife how much I love her and care about her everyday? Is it necessary to check on my parents throughout the week to see how they're doing? They live two blocks away! I need to show my friends I care about them too? Seriously? Bro. They're grown men.

Well, grown men or not, people prefer to be acknowledged and cared for. No matter how far away your parents are, they still worry about you... and themselves. They worry you may not be around to care for them, and more importantly, that they won't be around to care for you. Even if your parents are young and healthy, they just want to make sure you're okay. Imagine having someone else be a literal and figurative extension of you. Because that's what we are – we're are an extension of our parents. From blood, genes, and chromosomes to family name, habits and reputation. Ali remembers as he was growing up, the pride that would glow on his dad's face whenever Ali did something well. It could be getting an "A" in Social Studies, making the perfect golden crust pizza, or even swatting a fly at the first try. "*Ibn Abooh!*" Ali's dad would say. *His father's son!* Though Abu Ali, Ali's father, was so proud of his son's achievements, Ali was just as proud to be 'his father's son'.

But, what if Abu Ali never showed Ali how much he cared? What if Ali's parents never spent the time with their kids to help them achieve their goals and be there to positively reinforce their good behavior? Well, things might have turned out different. "I know it would have been different. I would not be the person I am today without the care of my parents, first and foremost, and help of my mentors and friends," Ali says. Beyond being positive with one another and encouraging each other to do good things, displaying 'care' is part and parcel to molding who we are as individuals.

Imam Ali tells us that if we love our brother we should tell them we love them. Share your love with your family and friends. Express yourself and let them know how important they are to you. It really is important. No matter how much you think that someone *already* knows how you feel, it's different when you hear it. Think about it. God gave us an entire book of His own words, telling us how much He cares. He sent us thousands of prophets, from Adam to Muhammad, to guide us because He cares about us. If caring wasn't so important, then why does God show us how much He cares all the time?

COMPASSION TO ALL

In the last chapter we mentioned the eve of Ashura, when Imam Hussain gathered all of his companions. When he told them that they were free to leave during the night, they refused to leave his side. He told them that he would not blame them for leaving him. He emphasized that the Umayyads only wanted him dead. It was not their fight, he stressed. Still, they wouldn't move an inch. They saw that their leader dug his boots in the ground, so they did the same.

They wouldn't leave him, they couldn't. They were wired differently. Loyalty became apart of who they were, each and every one of them. "We will never leave you," they said. "For you a thousand times over." They wouldn't stop saying it. Like a personal prayer they repeated. *A thousand times over.*

You'll see that the compassion in Ashura is not isolated in one or two incidents, it's a constant theme. On the day of Ashura, Imam Hussain would come out to the battlefield and call on to the people in the Umayyad army. He pleaded with them not to spare his life but to save their own souls. "If you have no faith and do not fear the Day of Judgment, then at least be free in this world of yours..." The Umayyads would have nothing of it. He called on deaf ears, ones that wished to hear nothing of truth or salvation. It pained the Imam to see people with such black hearts. It pained him to see that the nation of his grandfather had come to such a point. The Imam valued life, spoke of its sanctity, and wished to protect it at all costs. It was only at this brink, in which the nation was on the verge of complete corruption and the identity of the faith was at risk of total compromise, that the Imam said with lion-like confidence, "If the religion of Muhammad will not remain intact except by my death, then o' swords take me."

Imam Hussain shows us that he did not wish ill on anyone, even his enemies. He called on to them and urged them to reconsider the crimes they wished to commit. He prayed for them. He was in pain *for* them. Of course, when they were adamant and showed no signs of retreat, remorse or hesitation, he fought them until his last dying breath. Like his father Imam Ali, he defended the faith and gave his life to protect the principles of justice and freedom. Nonetheless, he tried everything in his power to show those on the other side compassion and mercy. We must do the same. We must guide others with compassion. Imagine being the light that people follow. But know the purpose of light and why it shines. The light doesn't shine so people can see, it shines because that's what light does. That is what Imam Hussain did – he shined, not with the desire to have people follow him but by the mere fact that he was a manifestation of God's guiding light.

FORGIVE TO BE FORGIVEN

We have all been hurt in some way during our lives – young and old. For our youth, you may think you're going through the worst problems ever right now. Worst. Life. Ever. Something like that? Don't worry it doesn't get any better. Just kidding. It actually does, because you'll realize the problems you were going through when you were a teenager are so insignificant to the problems you'd be facing now as an adult. The Adult-You will see the real life responsibilities of being married, raising a family, paying a mortgage, avoiding paying your grad school debt (Debt? What debt?), and trying to be a decent human being to strangers and family all at the same time. You'll look at your teenage years and wish they would stay forever. But they won't. They can't. Nothing does. So, forgive.

Forgive those that have wronged you. No matter how badly you were hurt, forgive. We know that can be tough at times because people can be really mean, rude, hurtful, basically plain-old evil. Truth is, so can we. By 'we', we don't mean us the authors – we mean all of us, including you. Yes, you. We have all done things that we regret. We all have our mistakes and shortcomings. Just as others have hurt us, we have most definitely hurt others. "Me? Never!" Please. Give us a break. What is worse than sin is being blind to it. Joking aside, we hope that the reader thinks long and hard about the people they've hurt. "But that's so negative, why would I do that?" Think about it like this. As human beings, we generally like praise and to be thought of positively by our peers. If you want to increase the chances of you being seen in a positive light then you ought to have a strategy that works. "I got it. Anytime I do something good I'll show it off to the world on Facebook, Twitter, YouTube, Instagram, Snapchat, WhatsApp, and maybe even buy some Google ads!" No. Please no. If you're already a social media fanatic, please calm down with your personal/spiritual life posts. It may be inspirational to others to an extent, but at other times it can just be wrong.

Back to that strategy. Why not employ an internal checking system? It's simple. Anytime someone does something good to you, write it down. Remember it. Associate that person with the good they did to you. Ok, sounds great. Now, anytime someone does something bad to you, don't write it down. Why not? We don't want you to harbor negative thoughts about that person. Remember you can't control their behavior. You can only control your own. So, don't write it down. Instead, acknowledge the wrong but forgive them for it. Next, whenever you do something good to someone... "Write it down right?" No. Don't write it down. What? Why not? Didn't we just write down the good stuff that the other people did to us? Yes. But we don't want ourselves to get bigheaded. Now, when we do something wrong then write it down. By employing this type of practice we can ensure two things.

One, we will inadvertently gravitate people towards us because of our good conduct. Remember though, intention is key. If our intention in all of this is just to get people to like us, we won't fare too well. People can smell disingenuity from a mile away. Don't be fake. Two, we will be striking a much needed balance in ourselves between humility and progress. That balance will allow us to forgive others. Always remember the good that people do to you and never forget the wrong that you have done to others. We will come to realize that we need to forgive to be forgiven by others, and ultimately for God to forgive us. If we keep track of the wrong that we do, not even against other people just between us and God, we may need more than one notebook to keep track. By such a realization, we find it not only rational to forgive others but the only logical step forward for our own salvation and success.

BE CONSIDERATE

Contrary to what many people think, it's not always great to be right. More importantly, it's not so great to always *want* to be right. We're not talking about being on the path of truth and righteousness, understanding your purpose, not committing injustices... that's all great. We're talking about arguments, disputes, disagreements. You and your brother, your spouse, your daughter, your colleague – whoever it is – get in an argument and you simply *have* to be right. That can really get exhausting.

First off, never start with "Let me tell you how you're wrong." Even if you are actually right, do you think the other side wants to hear it when you're coming off like that? Fine, I'll be calm. Yeah, sure. Let us know how that works. Instead of trying to shove your perspective down the other person's throat, why not try something new?

People don't like to be told they're wrong. In fact, people don't like to be wrong. We are all victims of that reality. Unless we change our perspective to be more encompassing of others and possibly give others a chance, we're not going to get anywhere in our 'debates' – more like an angry mob of English soccer fans. Have you seen those guys? They really are something else. Hats off to the Queen! Oh and sorry British readers, it's hard for us to say 'football' even though the rest of the world does. Speaking of Brits, Americans, and soccer we were sitting with a group of friends from England when an argument struck on soccer/football. The whole argument was on the use of the term 'soccer' by Americans as an invented, senseless term given that the whole world calls the sport football. The entire 'debate' was mostly in jest even though some of the guys were really passionate. The American guys started chanting USA! USA! USA! And the British chaps began singing praise to their Queen. It got quite out of hand.

All in all, it ended in laughs and the guys went on to a more useful subject. But there's some merit to mentioning this story. No one in the group conceded to understanding, or at least having a willingness to understand, the other side's perspective. Of course it was mostly jokes and laughs, but in seriousness each side held strongly to their perspective and didn't budge. Had the conversation been more serious the impact would have been more felt. Sticking with the sport example though, is it not easy to accept that there is another perspective outside of the American one? Absolutely, it's the perspective of the practically the rest of the world. Australia agrees with us though.

And is it not reasonable that the Brits understand that we use the word soccer for their 'football' because our football is an original American sport that is arguably the most popular sport in our country? Soccer is an afterthought for us, unfortunately. And though the popularity of soccer may be on the rise in recent years, the fact remains that it is not football to us. This is based on our experiences and choices as a culture, as a people, as a nation. A bit serious for soccer? Maybe. But we hope it drives the point. There are different perspectives out there. It's not about being right in these situations; it's more important for us to seek to understand one another. We may actually learn a thing or two.

LISTEN AND SEEK TO UNDERSTAND

Let's give a little more attention on seeking to understand. Here are a few tips that have helped us tremendously.

First, don't interrupt others when they are talking. In fact, don't try to finish their sentences either. "I know what you're going to say." No, you don't. And even if you do, it's rude. "But I don't want to waste time." Imagine someone told you to stop talking because they thought it was a waste of time. How would you feel? Pretty bummed out. It's not cool. Contrary to what we may think, other people can actually be more knowledgeable and more enlightened than we are.

That goes to our second tip. Pretend that everyone is knowledgeable except you. Try it. Suppose you don't have the answers and other people do. They may be right, they may be wrong. Still, they could have a perspective that may benefit you. Imagine having that humility and humbleness. You are consciously trying to learn from the people around you, from their experiences, expertise and wisdom. For more on humbleness, refer to chapter 4.

Third, make it a priority to be a better listener. Tips one and two automatically help you in doing that. Make a conscious effort to listen more and talk less.

Imam Ali tells us, "He who speaks more commits more errors. He who commits more errors becomes shameless. He who is shameless will have less fear of Allah. He whose fear of Allah is less, his heart dies. He whose heart dies enters the Fire." So, talking less is a good idea for all of us.

Four, take a deep breath before you speak. Tip number three doesn't mean we shouldn't speak, it just means we should practice listening more. Being a better listener makes us better speakers – even better public speakers, in fact. When we listen more we are able to retain more. We learn more by listening. Think of speaking like output – a stereo, a radio, the speaker on your phone, your laptop, or a stage. Listening is like input – a recording device. It takes in all the information needed. Without the recording you won't have any output. Our favorite shows and movies were recorded and then broadcasted. In order to have output, in order to broadcast, you have to record. You need input. And the better the input, the better the output. The better we listen the better we speak. So, breathe before you speak. Recall what you know, and if you don't have enough to give then speak in a way that initiates learning instead of presumptuous teaching.

Finally, remind yourself of where you come from. This never fails. And by where you come from, we're not just talking about where you're "*from from*" like the Middle East, Europe, or South Asia. Go way back. True reality. At the end we realize that no matter what, no matter where we are in our journey to God – we always go back to Him. "And here I am running away from You only to go back to You..." Back to You my Lord, *back to You.*

Six

Be Thoughtful

A Father's Letter

My son,

I think of you often. I feel your presence even though you are still to be born. I think of the days that I will spend with your mother, ensuring that she is cared for so that she may take care of you. You're in her womb now, she protects you in a way that no one else can protect you. These days I fall deeper in love with your mother because of you. I know it. I think of the days when I will hold you in my arms. When I will see you grow and be the proudest a man can be. I think of you often.

I think of all the wrong I have done and all the right. I pray that I can be a model for you. That you can take the right I have done and make it better and avoid the mistakes I made during my youth. This life is so delicate and so impressionable. Be wise. Do not experience things for the sake of the experience. Save yourself and heed to good counsel, and the best counsel is your Lord. He speaks to you, He speaks to all of us. His word is eternal. His ambassadors are immortal.

My son, my statements may not make much sense to you but I want you to think deeply. Before you act, before you do anything at all, I want you to think deeply. Do not fall for desire. Do not fall for the carnal weakness of our flesh. Be proud. Think of your name. Think of where you come from. Think of your heritage. Raise your head high but not to lower the heads of others. Be humble. They work together if you equate pride to confidence and humility to piety. If pride becomes arrogance it is disbelief, and if humility becomes insecurity it is weakness. We are not weak and we are not small. We are bigger than life...

Sincerely,

Your father

REFLECT

Imagine Imam Hussain as he held his newborn Abdallah, only 6 months old, in his arms walking out into the battlefield. Why was he taking him to the battlefront? "Some water for this child," he called out to the people that had killed his brothers, sons, and companions. "The dispute is between the adults. What is the crime of this newborn baby?" He held his child in his arms so that they could all see his thirst. His little eyes sunk back from dehydration. His lips parched and his skin dry as sand. The Umayyad camp went into disarray. Half saying, "Give him water!" The other half calling out, "Let the kid die with his father!" The dispute was ended though very quickly. Harmala, a fierce archer, would aim for a particular target. Did he want to kill Imam Hussain and orphan this newborn? No. He hit the target he wanted. Not the neck of Hussain, but the small neck of Abdallah. The blood gushed from his little lifeless body, and his thirst was finally quenched.

Thus far, you have probably come to realize an underlying theme in this book: reflection. That is the particular focus of this chapter. When we reflect we allow ourselves to expand our minds using the things that we see, hear, feel and interact with on a daily basis. To reflect is to give deeper meaning to things. It is to appreciate what is and be thankful for what isn't. Contemplation gives us a new dimension to purposeful living and actually is the key to making a meaningful life possible. The ability to contemplate what has passed, what is currently taking place, and what might become of ourselves and the world is an intellectual faculty that is arguably unmatched in value. Without having the ability to contemplate, our lives become dull, colorless and lacking.

Prophet Muhammad said, "An hour of contemplation is better than 70 years of worship." The very thought of this is breathtaking. The Prophet's word is the word of God. When he tells us something, he means it. Imagine standing on a prayer rug for 70 years worshiping God and singing His praises. Now sit down for an hour and contemplate on your life.

Think about the things that you have done – the good and the bad. Evaluate your strengths and weaknesses. Assess what you need to change and how your repentance from your bad habits, this time, will actually be effective. Those 60 minutes right there are the same as those 70 years. We're not saying it, the Prophet is. In fact, he's saying they're better than the 70 years not just the same.

God tells us in the Holy Quran, "Do they not reflect within themselves? God did not create the heavens and the earth and what is between them two but with truth...."[24]

God points to His creations – the heavens, the earth, and everything in between – and tells us to reflect on their very existence. He is giving us guidance to look at everything we have in life and ponder. Even the simplest things warrant our thought and contemplation.

And when reflecting on all these things, let's look at ourselves and think. God says, "Do they not reflect within themselves?" This reflection within ourselves is an introspection to see who we are and what is our position in the world we live in. That reflection is essentially an opportunity for us to see where we are at and where we are going. Setting time aside to reflect on our purpose, our goals, our aspirations and

---

[24] The Holy Quran, 30:8.

our progress is crucial. Our progress? What is this a status report for work? Nope. It's a progress report for life. Let's set aside a few minutes a day and think about how we are spending our lives. In 10 years, we'll be thankful we did.

This should be daily routine. Just like brushing our teeth, washing our face, and eating breakfast – contemplation is that fundamental. We should try not to neglect contemplation as an activity that we decide to do once in a blue moon. It has to become a routine and integral part of our daily lives. Set aside quiet time every day and think. Reflect. Be selfish with that. You deserve it. You need it. We all do.

Try this. Look at what's around you. If you're indoors you can look at the things inside, but if you can go outside for a minute do so. Open your door and step outside.

"It's a cool, breezy, Sunday morning in early October. The sun is barely showing, veiled by the clouds. Are the clouds protecting us from the sun or protecting the sun from us? Maybe we took the sun for granted this summer and wished it away? We can be quite ungrateful at times. I wish the clouds wouldn't take us so seriously. The leaves are falling too quickly, and yet so slowly. They fall with a grace that only God can give. The colorful leaves - red, yellow, orange, brown, some even with a little

hint of green – dance in the wind. As if there was a little fiesta taking place right in front of me, just for me. I remember the days when we would rake the leaves and launch each other into the piles of red and orange. We would play until dark. We would laugh. We would smile. We were innocent. We loved life and life loved us. It doesn't seem to be the same. I thought fall was supposed to end and other seasons follow. It seems that every year for me has been a deeper and deeper fall. That needs to change. I need to change. I'll grow back my leaves, and maybe I'll make sure my fall never comes again."

This could be on your morning commute to work or school. Maybe you can set aside five minutes after you pray just for contemplation. Take the time to think. Five minutes could be worth hours, days, or even years in worship. To repeat the saying of our Holy Prophet, "An hour of contemplation is better than 70 years of worship."

But what exactly should we reflect about during this time? You may be thinking to yourself, 'I always think during my morning commute. I think about my work schedule, my colleagues, and what I packed for lunch. How many years of worship does that equal?'

That's not the type of thinking we are talking about here. Clearly, for our thoughts to be equated to years of worship there must be something really significant that we should be thinking about. It's not just thinking about the humdrum tasks of everyday life. It is deeper than that. We are deeper than that. We need to be thinking of something bigger. What is it that we should be reflecting on, then?

The Commander of the Faithful Imam Ali said, "Blessed is he who knows where he came from, where he is at, and where he is going." Know where you came from. Know where you are at. Know where you are headed. Know your past. Know your present. Know your future. Know your origin. Know your purpose. Know your goal.

Think of your habits and mistakes. Some of us may have a problem with anger or patience. Some of us may have a problem with foul language or backbiting. Some of us may have a problem with modesty and controlling our gaze. With each of these, we need to first identify the problem. We need to look at ourselves and our past and realize that we have an issue that needs to be addressed. We then need to know where we need to be. We need to set goals for ourselves to improve and better ourselves. And throughout this journey to better ourselves, we always need to be mindful of our development. We need to look at our current position and assess our progress towards the goals we have set.

Think of your problems as potential teachers. We all make mistakes. But what makes us grow is the ability to realize our mistakes and learn from them. We need to turn our regret or guilt for our past mistakes to the fuel for our progress and betterment moving forward.

HE'S EVERYWHERE

Of course, one of the most important things to reflect and contemplate upon is God – our creator and the creator of everything around us. Everything goes back to Him, and we must continuously contemplate His grace and be grateful for all His blessings. Otherwise, we will become heedless, neglectful, and forgetful.

God says in his Holy Book "But the god of you all is the One God: there is no god but He; He comprehends all things in (His) knowledge."[25] His knowledge and presence encompass everything. No matter how much we distance ourselves from God through our sins and misdeeds, He will always be there. He will be there to judge us for all our actions.

---

[25] The Holy Quran, 20:98.

And He will be there to accept us when we turn back to Him in repentance.

In trying to repent, this reflection was shared with us:

"I'm lost to this sin, to this desire, to this hunger, to this darkness. I have no control. I have no mind in those instances. So powerful, I can't decide simply because I only have one choice - to feed in to the weakness, to fall to my lowest low, to lose everything. The feeling is strong in the moment. Then it weakens, but remains eerie in my heart and soul. Almost like a coma, where I'm still alive and breathing but I can't appreciate the things in midst. Then my mind awakes and reprimands me for disabling it. I accuse it of not protecting me, that I was the victim and I am still in the right. I victimize and oppress myself only to rise and say that I was the victim and oppressed. Which in reality is the truth. I am the oppressor of myself and I am my own victim. It's become so repetitious really. I feel locked up, and I can't get out and be free. I can escape for a while but only to return to the same paralyzing feeling and lack of control. I feel so sick... so sick of myself. I don't feel worthy to turn to Him, but feel guilty because I don't. Wherever I turn, He is there. And if I wish to run away, I will only be headed back to Him. For whichever direction I take He was and is always there.

"Am I a thief? Stealing my own time away from the potential that is me? If so, oh self forgive me. I'm not as mature and competent as you would like me to be. I would like to be better. I really do. But do I? You tell me. What have you seen of me? Have you seen anything good? Yes. Without consistency though. I'm telling you I'm continually interrupted. That's the issue. Excuses. I'm sorry. No excuses. Just forgive me. I'm unworthy of forgiveness, but You are the most gracious. I'm unworthy of anything actually, but You deserve all praise and gave everything to everything when no thing deserved anything. Forgive me. Don't take me back until I am as You want me... Your servant."

A man by the name of Dhi'lib al-Yamani once asked Imam Ali if he had ever seen God. The Imam replied, "Would I worship a god that I have not seen?" Dhi'lib asked, "How do you see Him?" The Commander of the Faithful replied, "Eyes cannot see Him as they see visible things, but the hearts perceive Him through the reality of faith."

So what do we mean when we say that God is *everywhere*? The Imam tells us that God is not seen through the eyes. Rather, He is 'seen' – His existence is realized – through the heart and the mind. If we spend the time contemplating upon the things that God has created, we will see God with the eye of our intellect. If we have faith and believe in God, reflecting on all His blessings over us, we will see God with the eyes of our heart.

GOD'S RIGHTS

In his invaluable book *A Treatise on Rights*, Imam Ali Al-Sajjad describes the rights that everything has upon the individual. He starts, of course, with the most important right – the right that God has over us and our duties toward Him.

The Imam says, "The greatest right of God against you is that you worship Him without associating anything with Him." As we mentioned before, the greatest sin in Islam is that of ascribing partners to God. God himself says, "Indeed God does not forgive that partners should be ascribed to Him, but He forgives anything besides that to whomever He wishes. Whoever ascribes partners to God has indeed fabricated [a lie] in great sinfulness."[26]

Of course, associating others with God does not stop at idolatry or worshiping any God beside the One True God of Prophets Abraham, Moses, Jesus, and Muhammad. Association with God can extend to far less obvious modes of thought and behavior. When a person can only think of money, he associates wealth with God. When a person can think of noth-

---

[26] The Holy Quran, 4:48.

ing but their video games, their music, and their celebrities, they've associated them with God. When God had brought us into existence but we are ungrateful and do nothing to thank Him, we have associated others with God.

When God gives us a clear command and we fail to follow, we have ascribed a partner to God. How so? God clearly tells us to lower our gaze and reel in our carnal desires. What are we doing when we disobey this command? Essentially, we are giving precedence to our carnal desires over the word of God. We are placing our desires in a position equal to or greater than that of God's commands. This is clearly an instance of ascribing partners to God.

Or take for example a person that is so entrenched in the world of music and musicians that they know every song in a given genre. Many people dedicate so much time to their music that they begin to memorize the lyrics of the songs. They dedicate so much time to the musicians that they know their life inside and out.

Isn't it a clear problem when a person memorizes the lyrics for volumes of music, but does not memorize more than a couple short chapters of the Quran? Isn't it a clear problem when a person knows more about musicians than they know about our prophets and imams? So how do we address these issues?

Let's go back to the words of Imam Al-Sajjad. The Imam continues, "When you do that [i.e. worship God] with sincerity, He has made it binding upon Himself to give you sufficiency in the affairs of this world and the next." God makes to us a promise – and when He makes a promise, He surely delivers. God promises that if you worship Him with sincerity, He will provide for you. He will take care of your problems. He will continue to bless and sustain you.

This also means that you should have complete reliance on God. We should rest at ease knowing that He will continue to bless us with His sustenance and suffice us through His mercy. And this doesn't stop with this world. The Imam tells us that so long as we worship God with sincerity, then He will suffice us in the hereafter.

DEATH AND BEYOND

Many people have a very negative view of death. They see it as a great catastrophe. They see it as the end. But in fact, death is only a beginning. It is an inevitable reality that everyone will die. We will all eventually die. We cannot avoid it. And it is the beginning of a journey toward another life. But if death is such an inevitable reality, shouldn't we spend some time reflecting on its consequences. Imam Ali tells us that, "Whoever anticipates death will hasten towards good deeds."

If we truly realize that death is an inevitable reality and reflect on it, it will drive us to become better human beings. It will drive us to focus on and fix our shortcomings. It will drive us to help other people who are in need. It will drive us to think about God and what we can do to gain closeness to Him during our brief lives in this world.

Of course, it is natural to fear death. We should not be embarrassed of that reality. Human beings, by their nature, fear the unknown. They are discomforted when they realize that they are ignorant about something or are in the dark when it comes to a certain situation. But it is up to us to keep this fear in the forefront of our minds and make the thought of death a driving force for our advancement.

Imam Ali beautifully says, "I wonder at him who has forgotten death although he sees people dying. I wonder at him who denies the second life although he has seen the first life. I wonder at him who inhabits this transient abode but ignores the ever-lasting abode."

How can we forget about death when we see and hear of people dying all the time? We pass our condolences to our neighbors and our friends when their loved ones pass away, but we do not think that it will inevitably be us in that casket one day. How can we live in this world but deny the existence of the next? How can we look all around us and see the magnificence of God's creation, but think that it cannot be brought back to life just as it has been created the first time.

How can we live in this world but deny the Day of Judgment in the hereafter? How can we make use of God's blessings and sustenance and then claim that He will not judge us for our actions.

You see, the Imam is giving us a standard of balance that we must live by in this world. He does not tell us to overwhelm ourselves with the thought of death that we stop ourselves from living. Rather, he is urging us to continue with our lives but to keep the thought of inevitable death at the forefront of our minds. He is urging us to savor and appreciate every moment because life's moments are short and limited. He is telling us that we must make sure that every moment of this short life must be put to good use in aiming towards everlasting life in the hereafter.

THE LOVE OF GOD

Do you remember when you first got engaged? Do you remember how you felt towards your fiancé?

The butterflies and the fireworks, the moments imagined, the perfect settings you picture... remember? Of course you do. For all the unmarried couples out there, have you ever had a crush? Let's set aside the issue of what is permissible and what is not when it comes to gender relationships for a moment and take the 'crush' example.

When a person has a crush, they become enamored with the other person. They begin to think about them day and night. They think about them whenever they sit down to eat and when they go to bed. In fact, it gets hard to actually fall asleep at night because of how much they think about their crush. You toss and you turn and you can't stop thinking about your crush. You can't wait for the next time that you will see them. Even if it is just for a minute – you would give anything for that minute.

Again, the example doesn't stop at your high school crush. If you're recently engaged or married, you have similar feelings towards your spouse. "I fell in love as soon as I laid my eyes on her..." Right? Well that's not love, that's called infatuation. But, nonetheless, it's a strong feeling. That infatuation can even be controlling in some regards. People get crazy when they're 'in love'. You would do anything for the person you love. Right? Absolutely. Even outside of the romantic realm of love and infatuation, we can recall a number of relationships that are core to our being encompassed by love. Our parents, our siblings (well, sometimes), our family and best friends – we love them. We all feel a great degree of love and devotion to our parents. We all love our siblings and cherish our close friends. Now step back for a moment.

How many of us have that same feeling towards God? Isn't God the one who blessed us with the ability to have feelings like this – to feel? Isn't He the one who created us and everyone we love? Isn't He the one who guided our paths and allowed us to see the people that we fell in love with, blessing us with a spouse that means the world to us? Isn't He the one who blessed us with parents that gave us life? So, can we say that we truly love Him just the same? God's love encompasses us all – it encompasses everything. But do we acknowledge it, cherish it, revere it? Do we long to speak with God? Do we miss hearing His Word?

Can we honestly say we are 'in love' with Him? Probably not. And that is where our realization needs to be. For someone that gave us everything, we ought to be giving a lot more attention and endearment back. Not for His sake, but for ours. Because no matter what, we can't repay Him and our love will never equate to His. He has what we call 'true love'. He gives without expecting anything in return. He forgives our worst mistakes. And even though we hurt

Him, betray Him, disrespect Him, He doesn't stop giving. His love is not dependent on what mood we're in. He loves us, truly. Endlessly.

Why are we not infatuated with our Lord? Why don't we have these same thoughts and feelings when it comes to our prayer, when we are set for an audience with our creator? We know God's love. Without being told about it, we feel it. It's the most wholesome, natural, intuitive thing we can experience. Because God's love is in everything. God's love *is* everything.

The Last Day of Our Life

So how do we put these thoughts in action? How can these realities have an impact on our lives? Here's a simple step towards doing this. You may have heard it before and it may sound cliché to some of you. But it really does reflect a great wisdom that we can live by.

Live this day as if it were your last.

You may be really young. You may be a healthy football player. You may be a young lady with a bright future. But how many young men and women die despite this? We all know a few. Whether it is in your neighborhood or on the news, you know or have heard of someone who has died young. We know that death is inevitable and that it can come at any moment. This is not meant to make your life gloomy. Instead, this should only add more vibrancy to life. If you live with the perspective that today can be your last chance at doing something great, then you will excel in every day of your life. If you live with the thought that each day could be your last day to do good, then you will be doing good every day.

And no matter what our age is, we must always keep this in perspective. We must live with the knowledge that death may come at any second, and that once it arrives there is no turning back. God says in the Holy Quran, "Until when death overtakes one of them, he says: Send me back, my Lord, send me back; haply I may do good in that which I have left. By no means! It is a (mere) word that he speaks; and before them is a barrier until the day they are raised."[27]

We need to reflect on these verses and put them at the forefront of our mind. We need to live in this world with the goal of having as little regret as possible on the day we die – so that we do not need to ask God to turn us back, and we are not left with this regret when our pleas are turned down.

So the thought of death should not be depressing. It should not be frightening. You shouldn't feel down

---

[27] The Holy Quran, 23:99-100.

or feel hopeless. Rather, the thought of death should be a driving force that allows us to excel throughout our lives. So let's seize the opportunity. Let's make use of every moment of our short lives and seize every opportunity to lead a great life in the service of God. As Imam Ali says, "Let everyone of you seize the opportunity when he is healthy before the time when he is sick, when he is young before he is aged, old and sick, [the opportunity] of his ease before he is poor, of having free time before he is busy, of being wealthy before being impoverished, of being present at home before he is away traveling, of being alive before his death."

A young bright soul shared with us this reflection, inspired by the saying of Imam Ali: "This world is but an hour..."

"Who am I? Who have I become? I sit teary-eyed looking at the question I ask myself and cannot think of an answer. Don't I know who I am? I did. I don't anymore.

I was my mother's daughter. I was proud, able. I was confident in the things I did and my head was always held high. I kept in remembrance of Him and He always stayed in my heart. I was so focused, so driven.

So, what's changed? What has led me here to question myself? Is it the petty pressures this life brings that have taken me away from what I find peace in? Is it the upcoming exams and the deadlines on the papers that make me believe that I don't have the ten minutes in my day to pray? Or is it the late nights coming home that keep me too tired to read a couple verses of Quran before I go to bed? Are these laws of life more important than His law's? It can't be. There is no law but Allah's.

I'm just so tired. I'm so tired of this fake world where we live for everyone besides ourselves; where another's approval is more important to us than His. This world where we dress, act, speak, live for them and whoever but not for Him. If that is the world I chose to live in, I want nothing more of it. I wish to be closer to Your warmth. Who else but You?

Life is not easy, I know this. It is not meant to be a ride on a downhill stream. You need to struggle to swim upstream if you want to get closer to Him. It's hard but I'm trying, and I can only try. My body is growing so tired from fighting this water. Instead of trying to swim, I think I let myself settle for treading water, doing the basics. I'm stuck in the same place and its only making me grow more and more tired, so why don't I move?! Why can't I just move and save myself before I get so tired that I cannot continue to tread, and so drown? My body is lethargic and I remain stagnant. When you're stagnant, why is it so hard to get up and move?

Because it's hard to make an effort when you feel so lost and so far from what you were. It's hard to get back up and take control of what was yours when you've left it in the hands of a thief.

There will come a day when all that you see as worries and stress, all your accomplishments, all your hard work, brainpower, efforts, endless nights working, everything we live for is just going to be ashes... like us. It's not going to matter what you wore at that wedding or what your G.P.A was in college. It's not going to matter who your friends were or what kind of car you owned. And that day, what do you have to show for yourself? What are you left with to take to the grave? The only things that matter are those which you can carry on to your grave.

'This world is but an hour.' Don't waste it on petty things.

As for You... I'm finding my way back to you."

Seven

Be a Friend

Our Inspiration

In all subjects and matters, we as individuals can seek the highest peaks of knowledge by knocking on the Gate of the Prophet, Imam Ali. The Holy Prophet Muhammad stated, "I am the City of Knowledge and Ali is its Gate; whoever wishes to enter the City, must enter it through its Gate." This statement alone creates a stipulation of our desire to reach the Prophet, and that stipulation is the Imam. If we want to reach and benefit from the Prophet we must go through the Imam. The Holy Prophet also advised us in saying, "Whoever wishes to see Adam in his knowledge, Noah in his piety, Abraham in his forbearance, Moses in his strength, and Jesus in his worship and devotion should look at Ali ibn Abi Talib."

The inspiration and wisdom that comes from the City of Knowledge is unmatched. That inspiration wasn't limited to the Prophet's words of revelation. In fact, God tells about the all-encompassing divine leadership of the Prophet stating, "... He is nothing but revelation." That individual, the greatest of God's creation, told his followers that his gate, the way to his city, the checkpoint of entrance to the university of life was his brother and closest companion, Ali. It's no surprise that Imam Ali was the Prophet's most trusted companion, special confidant, and closest friend. He was there for him whenever he needed him, and he never disappointed. Imam Ali's commitment to the Prophet was unwavering. The number of times he put his life on the line for the Prophet is unmatched. It was from that leadership that the supporters of Imam Hussain were raised. Looking at Ali, companions like Habib ibn Muthaher, Zuhair ibn Al-Qayn, and Muslim ibn Aqeel knew what loyalty and friendship really meant. They knew that friendship and brotherhood were not relationships of convenience. They knew that they would be tested. They not only stood by Imam Hussain, they died for him.

THE FRIENDS OF HUSSAIN

Many of Imam Hussain's companions were actually companions of his father Imam Ali. Some of them were even companions of his grandfather, Prophet Muhammad. Their friendship and loyalty was blind to age, status, or tribe. Through their friendship and loyalty to the Prophet, Imam Ali and consequently Imam Hussain, the companions were also friends to one another. Race, ethnicity, tribe, and social status were not factors in their friendship. They shared a love and dedication so sincere it was unbreakable. That love was the love for truth. That love was the love of Ali. "Ali is with the truth and the truth is with Ali," the Holy Prophet said. These companions revered their Prophet and did what any loyal follower and true friend would do, they trusted him. They trusted that the Prophet's word was the word of God. They knew that he did "not speak out of whim" and that he was "nothing but revelation." It was clear. It was simple. But sometimes only a handful of people see things so simply and so clearly. That is why we only see a handful of companions with Imam Ali after the death of the Prophet and only 72 warriors ready to give their lives for Imam Hussain in Karbala. It's because true friends are rare. They're like diamonds. What a loss it would be to have a diamond within reach and think it's only a rock like any other rock.

The friends of Hussain knew the diamonds in their midst. Habib ibn Muthaher knew the immaculate brilliance that was Hussain, and Hussain knew the unwavering loyalty of Habib. He was one of the close companions of Imam Ali. Imam Ali selected him as one of the Imam's most trusted and senior legionnaires. He would later be one of the chief Kufans to write to Imam Hussain calling on to him to come to Kufa. He helped rally a staunch number of supporters in Iraq ready to support the Imam. The masses would betray the companions that were readying the grounds for the Imam's arrival, and numerous companions were consequently captured and executed. Imam Hussain's ambassador to Kufa, Muslim ibn Aqeel, came in to Kufa to be met by over 18,000 supporters. Yes. There were nearly twenty thousand men that chanted the name of Imam Hussain as a display of allegiance before Muslim ibn Aqeel. With the coming of the ruthless Umayyad governor, Ubaydallah ibn Ziyad, things changed.

People were bribed, threatened, arrested and executed. Those thousands became a handful. And that handful was arrested and executed, except for the few that escaped and found Imam Hussain on his way to Karbala. When Muslim was finally captured, he was brought before the Umayyad governor Ibn Ziyad. Blood stained his clothes after fighting his way through dozens of the governor's soldiers. He stood before the leering tyrant who was too excited to have captured the ambassador of Hussain. There was a cold exchange between the two and it wasn't long before Ibn Ziyad ordered Muslim's execution. "Take him to the top of the palace. Sever his head and throw his body from the rooftop," Ibn Ziyad callously commanded his men. Unfazed by his imminent death he accepted his fate. Still, his tears would roll. Muslim didn't cry for himself. He cried for his master, his leader, his beloved, his friend – Hussain. That name was the last name that Muslim uttered. *Hussain.*

When news came to Imam Hussain that Muslim ibn Aqeel was executed, along with other companions like Hani ibn Urwa, the Imam's heart became heavy. At this point he went before the people and read the following:

'In the Name of God the Beneficent the Merciful. I have received tragic news. Muslim ibn Aqeel, Hani ibn Urwa, and Abdullah ibn Yaqtur were all murdered. We have been abandoned by our followers. Whoever of you wishes to leave now will not be blamed.'

People began to disperse, left and right, until only those who came with him from Mecca remained. He did this because he feared that those who had followed his caravan thought that he was headed to a land where he will become the certain ruler. He hated that they would follow him without knowing what they were truly headed to. He knew that if he delivered to them this news, only those who were most loyal and wished to die alongside him would remain."

On the day of Ashura, Imam Hussain chose Habib ibn Muthaher as the commander of the left flank of his battalion during the mobilization of his forces. Even before the battle commenced, Habib tried his utmost best to rally more forces for Imam Hussain. Near Karbala, there was a small community of people from Habib's tribe, Banu Asad. He was able to get 90 fighters from his tribe to mobilize at night. An

Umayyad force of 400 cavalry stopped them, however, right before they could get to Imam Hussain's camp. Habib couldn't get the Imam more fighters, but he gave him everything else he had including his own life. When Habib was finally killed on the battlefield of Karbala, Imam Hussain was devastated. It wasn't just the loss of a supporter, it was the loss of a true companion – a true friend.

MY CLIQUE

Birds of a feather flock together. Your friends are truly a reflection of who you are. Our religion puts a great emphasis on friendship and on spending time with the right people – being with the right crowd. We see this not only in the narrations given to us from the Imams, but exemplified through their actions as well. Habib, Muslim, Hani and the other companions of Imam Hussain – they were a reflection of the Imam. Though they were small in numbers, they were bigger than life. On the eve of Ashura, after Imam Hussain told his companions that they had his permission to take leave in the darkness of the night none of them moved an inch. They stood their ground in support of the man that meant more than the world and all it had to offer. To their unwavering loyalty Imam Hussain said, "I could not wish for a better group of companions."

We won't stop in this chapter with the normal conception of 'friendship' that we usually come across. We want to emphasize that friendship is a much stronger bond than most people think and it extends even to brotherhood and sisterhood. The relationship that you have with your friends must likewise extend to the people that are most close to you. Every one of us needs to treat their siblings and their family the way they treat their friends. Note that Imam Hussain's love and appreciation for his friends did not overshadow his adoration for his brother Abbas, his son Al-Akbar, or his daughter Sukayna. Like the Imam, we need to spend time and connect with both our friends and our family members alike. But more on that later.

On the subject of friendship, which affects all of us in numerous ways, we look toward the wisdom of the Commander of the Faithful. The Imam states, "Tell me who you befriend, I'll tell you who you are." If our very identity can be derived and shown by simply pointing and identifying who our friends are, it seems that at the very least who we befriend is something we should pay extra attention to. So friends are important. In fact they're more than important, they're essential to who we are. The Imam is telling us just that. Our friends are our mirror, people that we can look at and see a reflection of ourselves.

Before we can answer what kind of people we should befriend, the Imam gives us an outline of the kind of people we *shouldn't* take as friends.

WHO ARE MY FRIENDS?

During his last days, Imam Ali gave invaluable advice to his oldest son Imam Hassan. Imam Ali told his sons that that they should avoid four types of people, and he advised them on how to go about choosing friends. Of course, when the Imam is advising his sons he is not reserving that advice for Hassan and Hussain exclusively. The second and thirds imams very well knew the importance of friendship and who to take as companions. They accompanied their father in all his endeavors and emulated his every step. They were his shadow. They were a reflection of him. They were their father's sons. And as such, he would advise his followers through them.

Before we dive into this categorization Imam Ali provides, take a moment to reflect on the context of this guidance. Imam Ali is giving this advice to his sons while he is on his deathbed. How great of a topic does Imam Ali hold friendship to be that he is addressing this during the last moments of his life?

Imam Ali says, "Do not make friendship with a fool because when he will try to do you good he will do you harm." What exactly does Imam Ali mean by this 'fool'? Basically, a fool is a person whose mind isn't in the right place, who is immature and irresponsible. A juvenile. Hassan is studying for a big exam that he's sitting for tomorrow. It's about 9pm and he still needs a solid two-hour stretch to review his last set of notes. Ziyad calls Hassan at 9:30pm, interrupting his two-hour mission only a half-hour in. Hassan feels bad when he doesn't answer people's phone calls. "I would hate it if someone saw my name on their phone and didn't answer my call. If I see the call I have to answer," he says. "Hey! Hassan!" Ziyad practically yelling through the phone. "What's up Ziyad?" "I just got my new car from the dealer an hour ago. Let's go for a ride. We'll get some milkshakes and hang out or something. You down?" Hassan replies, "I got a big exam tomorrow I'm studying for. Maybe over the weekend *inshallah*." "Bro. You're already pretty smart, you don't need to study. *Khaye*, we'll get whatever you want. We can go racing too!"

Ziyad probably doesn't mean Hassan any harm, but if Hassan takes him up on his offer he's going to be hurting himself. One, if he doesn't continue studying he is going to hurt his chances at doing well on his exam. Two, if Ziyad does decide to race some other hothead on the street he's unnecessarily putting himself in a dangerous situation. Now some of us may be thinking, 'What's the big deal to put the pedal to the medal every once in a while?' Would you ask that same question to the families of the thirty thousand people that died in car accidents last year? Probably not. It's not strange that people commonly say, "It's better to be safe than sorry." It really is. Similarly, Hassan would be better off safe than sorry. "Have fun Ziyad, but I'm good."

Imam Ali continues, "Do not make a miser your friend because he will run away from you at the time of your dire need." Don't be friends with a cheapskate. A person who is a miser, someone who is cheap with their time and money, is someone that will likely sell you out when you need them most. And even they don't sell you out they won't be there for you when others aren't there to help you. There were a lot of misers out there that deserted Imam Hussain and did not come to his aid. Some betrayed him – the sellouts. Others didn't even show up. Both groups were misers.

The Imam is not simply speaking about people who are miserly when it comes to money and finances. We see that our Imams took as companions those who were willing to sacrifice for them, as the were Imams ready to sacrifice for their companions.

The best example of this is the companions of Imam Hussain. Those companions sacrificed their lives on the lands of Karbala in protection of Imam Hussain.

They were not forced to be there and give up their lives. In fact, Imam Hussain would constantly warn them along the way that they were headed towards a battle where they will be sacrificing their lives. Even on the eve before the battle he gave them a chance to leave and save their lives. But for Hussain's sake, they stayed. They sacrificed. They lived and died with him, for him.

So if your friend is not willing to put things on the line for you and sacrifice for you, then why should you invest your time with them? Why should you be giving your time and investing in a relationship in which the other side will not put in the same effort?

Going back to Imam Ali's advice, he says "Do not be friendly with a vicious and wicked person because he will sell you and your friendship at the cheapest price." You need to be observant of people and see the way they act.

Don't be friends with a prankster that will demean and degrade others just because it's fun. If someone gets personal pleasure from hurting other people, there's something wrong there. We can't blanket things with the excuse of 'just messing around' all the time. 'Messing around' can ruin people's lives. We can't be friends with someone who is willing to ruin another individual's reputation or career. Even if they don't go the extent of ruining the person's reputation or career, they may do similar damage through mockery. Don't be friends with people who are constantly mocking others, because you will never know when these people will turn back and do the same thing to you. God tells us in Chapter 49 verse 11 of the Holy Quran: "O you who have faith! Let not any people ridicule another people: it may be that they are better than they are..."

Finally, Imam Ali says, "And do not make friend of a liar because like a mirage he will make you visualize very near the things which lie at a great distance and will make you see at the great distance the things which are near to you." Simply, don't befriend a liar because honesty isn't important to them. They will manipulate the truth, utilize lies, and mislead people to get their way. Your friend should be someone that you can trust. A friend should be someone that you can share your time with and make them a part of your life. But how can you trust a liar to be part of your life when the very foundations of the relationship could very well be based on... a lie.

Fools, misers, liars, and wicked people, stay away! We really can't afford the negative consequences that come with people of these characteristics. And if we happen to have some of these foolish, miserly, lying or wicked tendencies, we need to check ourselves real fast and start making some modifications in our personalities and behavior. Change is not bad, as long as it's in the right direction.

Moreover, the Imam tells us, "If a friend envies you, then he is not a true friend." There's a big difference between a friend who is a little jealous because you got a new car while they're stuck with their old clunker, and a 'friend' who wished lightning would strike a large tree and crash perfectly into your new ride. Jealousy can easily develop into envy, which doesn't stop at wishing to have what your friend has but goes the next step to wanting what they have and wishing they didn't have it.

Picking your Friends

Knowing what kind of people that wouldn't be the best of friends, we can move on to the next question: so who is a good friend? Not only that, but who would be a true friend? Imam Ali tells us that "A true friend is one who sees a fault, gives you advice and who defends you in your absence." A true friend doesn't ignore your faults just to be polite. They are empathetic to your situation but are nonetheless honest and straightforward. And when they go forward to give you advice, it's not simply an arbitrary characterization of the situation; rather, it would be based on founded principles and solid models of conduct (i.e. a true friend would advise by contemplating, "What would the Prophet do in this situation?"). Moreover, that same true friend won't only be positive and kind to you in your presence, but will defend you in your absence as well. It's so easy to find a group of 'friends' socializing and bringing up the name of another peer (absent from the gathering) and nonchalantly mock them in the context of other jokes. Instead of laughing it off, a true friend would make a point to defend the absent friend and show that things like that are not appreciated.

Some might say, "You know what? I don't really need friends. I don't need to deal with people's drama and problems, and I won't get into any kind of trouble, headache, or heartbreak. Some may call me a loner or something negative like that, but I like riding solo." Well, avoiding a problem doesn't necessarily solve it. The Imam has given us advice to stay away from certain types of friends because of the negative affects that come with them. However, he doesn't advise us to let go of friendship altogether. Rather, the Imam states that a "lack of friends means stranger (*ghareeb*) in one's own country." Imagine going away on vacation or business for a week outside of the country and coming back home. Home just doesn't seem like home anymore and you feel like a complete stranger in your own country. Take it a step further. Imagine walking in to your house or apartment and not recognizing anything inside. Everything has changed, and you no longer feel like it's home. That's what lack of true friendship is.

Imam Ali says, "Unfortunate is he who cannot gain a few sincere friends during his life." Sincerity is the most important quality to look for in a friend. Sure, your friend may have a few flaws. Who doesn't? The Imam isn't telling us that we should only befriend people who are perfect. Yes, there are a few types of people that we should stay away from. But when choosing friends, the most important quality to look for is sincerity.

The Imam continues, "More unfortunate is the one who has gained them and then lost them (through his bad deeds)." Sincerity is so important in a friend that once we find someone with that quality we shouldn't let go. Just as the Imam instructs us to find friends who are sincere, so too we have to be sincere with our friends.

Friendship is a two way street. We expect our friends to be trustworthy, kind, generous, and responsible. We should reflect those same qualities. More importantly, just as we expect our friends to be sincere with us, we need to be sincere with our friends.

WHAT'S A FRIEND?

Now some of you might be thinking 'why all these restrictions?' 'So I don't hang out with the most generous people; what's the big deal?' 'Why does someone need to be kindhearted to be part of my movie-night crew?' Friends aren't just people that you hang out with, grab a meal with, or chat with on a regular basis. A true friend is someone that is invested in your growth, just as you are invested in theirs. Friendship is a relationship of mutual care, respect, and support.

Keep this in mind when you're spending time with your friends. What is each of you gaining from this time together? Are you just killing time? Or are you invested in each other's growth? What kind of conversations are you having about lunch? Are you just talking about football? Or are you talking about each of your goals and aspirations and helping each other reach their potential?

And you can't say that "I just hang out with them, that doesn't change who I am." That they don't reflect who you are. Friends are part of your life. Your friends are part of who you are. And that is partially because they affect how you behave. Let's say that you are hanging out with your team after practice one day. Or you're hanging out with colleagues after work. The sun goes down and prayer time hits. What do you do? What will your friends do?

Will you be the only one that thought of your prayer? Sometimes you know that your friends won't care and that in itself will discourage you from standing out from the pack and mentioning prayer. And if you have particularly bad friends, they will try to tell you that it's not a big deal and discourage you from your prayer all together. Spend enough time with a clique like that and you personally won't remember that prayer anymore. The group mentality will desensitize you and you will go with the flow without even realizing it.

Making good friends and keeping them is not an easy thing. It's a struggle. In high school, in college, and in the workplace, the struggle remains the same. But it's worthwhile. To have friends that will help you grow, and for you to be able to help them grow – it is a marvelous thing.

YOU CAN'T PLEASE EVERYONE

And keep in mind that you simply can't please everyone. Not everyone has to be your friend. A friend calls you up late at night and invites you to a night at the cigar club. You don't have to say yes. People around you will push and pull. Someone may want to hang out and gossip all day. Another may want to show off his muscles and his muscle car at the mall. Another will want you to watch the football game instead of focusing on that exam or that tight deadline that's coming up.

You just can't please everyone. You will have to say no. And if you're saying no, then you might as well set a standard and stick by it. And the best standard is that given to us by our Imams – a friend is a person who will be sincere with you, care about you, and invest in your personal growth. And when you realize that you can't please everyone, you can really hone in on what is really important. The only one you should be looking to please is God – because He is the One that matters.

There's one really thought-provoking parable that we wanted to share here. Prophet Abraham was one of our great prophets. He was given the task of delivering God's message to a people that rejected God outright. But no matter how much Abraham preached, people rejected him. They made fun of him and insulted him for believing in the One True God. Despite all the trouble that these people put him through, he never hesitated in his divinely given mission. He never asked anything of anyone, but always turned to God for his needs.

Abraham had a habit of going out every day in search of the poor and the destitute so that he could provide them with a meal and help them in their lives. One day, Abraham went out on such a search but found no one in need of help. When he returned home, he was astonished to find a man in his house despite his door having been locked. He quickly asked the man, "By whose permission did you enter this house?"

The man quickly answered, "I entered by the permission of its owner." Though this answer might sound puzzling, Abraham understood exactly what the man meant. Yes, Abraham was the owner of the house – but the true owner of the house is the One God to whom everything owes its existence.

The man who had entered Abraham's house was none other than Archangel Gabriel, who had come down to Earth in the form of a human by God's command. When Abraham asked about the archangel's mission, Gabriel answered "God Almighty has sent me to one of His servants. He wants me to award him with the rank of al-Khalil, the Friend of God."

Joyous and eager, Abraham asked "I beg you to tell me who he is so I can serve him for the rest of my life." Gabriel smiled. He replied, "Abraham you are he... It is because you never asked anybody besides God for anything. And He never asked you for anything but that you said, 'Yes.'"

In essence, God was telling Abraham not to worry about the people that had rejected him and stood against him for so long. That even when you feel like you don't have friends, know that God is always there for you and that He is the only one you truly need.

DON'T FORGET ABOUT FAMILY

Most of us are very kind and nice to our friends. We spend a lot of time with them and hang around them almost every day. On the other hand, a lot of us have a problem with being nice to our siblings. Let's face it – sibling rivalry, fights, and bickering are so normal that they seem like the right and natural way to be with your family. And no matter how young or old, we have to keep our family close and make sure our relationship with our kin is as good as can be.

God says in the Holy Quran, "And when We made a covenant with the children of Israel: You shall not serve any but God and (you shall do) good to (your) parents, and to the near of kin."[28] Notice how God puts these three things together for us – serve God, be good to your parents, and be good to your relatives. Contemplate on this connection. Don't think that a person can be a good individual and a faithful believer without being good to his or her family.

---

[28] The Holy Quran, 2:183.

Build on it

To the younger siblings, Imam Al-Sajjad tells us "The right of him who is older than you is that you show reverence toward him because of his age and you honor him because he entered Islam before you." We never really think about this, but our older siblings have a head start advantage when it comes to the race to please God. They've been praying for longer than we have. They've been helping people for longer than we have. They've had a head start and they've been able to accumulate more experience and reach more of their potential because of it.

The Imam continues, "You leave off confronting him in a dispute, you do not precede him in a path, you do not go ahead of him, and you do not consider him foolish. If he should act foolishly toward you, you put up with him and you honor him because of the right of Islam and the respect due to it."

Some of us, especially when we are young, think that we know it all. We don't give our older siblings the time to talk to us and give us advice. But if you think that your brother is foolish, remember that he has been around for a longer time and has more experience to show for it. And even if your older brother or sister does something that is wrong, be patient and respectful because of their right over you.

So it is important to always be respectful to our elders. But our younger siblings also have a right over us. The Imam says, "The right of him who is younger is that you show compassion toward him through teaching him, pardoning him, covering his faults, kindness toward him, and helping him."

HOW TO MAKE FRIENDS

We love our family, but let's get back to friends. Now how do I make good friends? Be yourself. Be good and good people will surround you. Imam Ali said, "Justice and fair-play will bring more friends," and that "Cheerfulness is the key to friendship." So play nice, and smile. It really is as simple as that. Don't try to impress others or act out of your element, be yourself. But if you feel that you are not cheerful, just, or fair, then maybe you should use this contemplation as an opportunity to adopt some of these positive characteristics; not just to get friends, but because these characteristics are those of the prophets and the wise.

In the end, we try our best to remind ourselves that "there is enough light for those who wish to see." – Imam Ali.

Eight

Be Real

The Story of Qassim

The young Qassim was so proud to serve his uncle Imam Hussain. He practically begged Imam Hussain to let him enter the battlefield. Not caring about death or being slain, he wanted to defend the honor of his father, his uncle, his religion, and everything that he held dear. Imam Hussain couldn't bear to see his nephew killed. He was so young. The Imam continued to insist that it was a battle of the Umayyads against him alone. He therefore tried to have his family and friends depart to spare their own lives. But, like the companions, the most noble family entrenched their feet in the sand of Karbala. That new land would become home. Their bodies would be buried in that land, and they would be visited by lovers even a thousand years later. Lovers of truth, from all walks of life, would journey to Karbala. They do everyday.

What moved Imam Hussain to finally let Qassim enter the battlefield? Qassim brought his uncle a letter. We could imagine, as Imam Hussain opened that letter and saw the handwriting of his late brother Imam Hassan, what thoughts ran through his mind. Perhaps he thought of the days when they played together and jumped into the arms of the Holy Prophet in Medina. The Prophet would hold them so tight and kiss them a thousand kisses. They would playfully climb on his back and shoulders, they would laugh and smile. He would sit them in his lap as he taught the companions about the principles of faith.

Or perhaps he thought of more recent memories. Maybe he pondered on the days of civil war and the sedition of groups that strayed from their grandfather's path. The battles of Jamel, Siffin, and Nahrawan. Battles waged against their father Imam Ali, who was also the Caliph of the time. Battles they fought in. Battles they won. But people grew tiresome of truth and principle. Their father wouldn't allow for the spoils of war against fellow Muslims, even if they were in the wrong. Their father was assassinated for his firm principles. People grew tired of it. They couldn't stomach the sacrifice that came with the Prophet's message – a message that their father Ali swore with his life to protect. And he did just that. Hassan would do just the same.

Perhaps he went on to think of their final days together. When Imam Hassan lay on his deathbed, his body aching from the poison that penetrated his bloodstream. Already stabbed in the back by his own soldiers, he would be poisoned by his wife – the final blow to an Imam that was already so oppressed. Imam Hussain would hold his betrayed brother, aching for his pain. As Hussain would sit closer, we could imagine he tried not to shed a single tear. But he couldn't hold back. He loved Hassan so much. In his eyes, Hassan was his better half. In Hassan's eyes it was the other way around. Their humility was part and parcel to their immaculateness. "Hussain, there will never be a day like your day," Hassan would tell his brother.

Before Imam Hassan would pass, he called on his son Qassim. Such a beautiful young man he was. And as the poetry reads, it would be as if Imam Hassan would say,

> Qassim, my dear Qassim, come. I have a few words for you, just some. But these words you keep close. This here no one but you knows. On the 10th day, on Ashuraa. Your uncle Hussain, the son of Zahraa. Will face an army, thousands of bands. So many they will cover the lands...

> In their evil they will stand. Led only by Yazid's command. And here Islam will demand. A sacrifice to be made on that land. On that day you will represent me. You will rise to the occasion and be. The youngest warrior they will see. On that day you will represent me.

> They will undermine you for your age. But that will give you more time to gauge. The weaknesses in their ranks. Their minds will be on the banks. On that day your uncle will be alone. But you will be

there to atone. For my lack of presence shown. For you are my son, my flesh and bone.

You will do this for me my son. And you will stand tall and proud. For like you there are none. 'I am the Son of Hassan,' You shout it loud, You make me proud.

History will remember your name. And know that nothing was done in vain. Our Lord will raise you with me, and your grandfathers Muhammad and Ali. History will remember your name. And know that even with all the pain, there will be no day like that of Hussain. So you will be there for me, just the same.

And then the 10th day came. So many companions and Hashimites slain. Qassim would rise and rise again, toward his uncle Hussain he would begin. 'Let me enter the battlefield, like Abbas I will be your shield! Like Ali Al-Akbar I am your son, I will defend the faith I wont run!'

My dear Qassim, I believe in you. But I can't let you go.

After some moments in time, Qassim comes forth in his father's gear. He is standing tall with nothing to fear. To Hussain he comes closer... he comes near.

With the letter he approaches his uncle, and Hussain reads it with too many tears...

After the letter how could Hussayn deny, what could he say, how could he sigh... He looked at Qassim again and would see, the reflection of his brother Hassan ibn Ali

Hussain softly touched Qassim's head and looked on with a broken smile. Qassim hugged him and said, 'Uncle, worry not, I have my father's style...

Uncle Hussain, on this 10th day I have only one thing to say, Death is like honey to me. To die with you is to be free... I am here to make you and my father proud. I am here to let the whole world hear me and I will shout it, yes shout it loud! I am the son of Hassan ibn Ali! Let the whole world hear me!

My father is surely here today. His name will bring the enemies dismay. For I am Qassim, to my Lord I pray. To have the enemies hear me when I say

'I am the son of Hassan ibn Ali, and I defend Prince of the Free. And as young as I may be, I stand a warrior, a lover of Ali!'

Qassim fought and was martyred fulfilling what he believed to be his purpose. Doing the right thing. He answered the call. Recognizing what is right and doing it, no matter what. Though so young, he lived a more meaningful life than some who live well beyond their seventies. In slang terms, Qassim kept it real. He didn't shy away from sacrifice, responsibility and leadership. He was a real man. He was a true hero. He was a legend in his own right. Qassim the son of Hassan.

BEING IN THE EYE OF THE STORM

We have all had our fair share of anxiety. Imagine turning on the television and the first thing that pops on the screen is, "Good evening ladies and gentlemen. Please do not leave your homes this evening. There are developments in the weather forecast for an unusual storm and a high chance of a tornado hitting Jackson City." You live in Jackson City. Time to freak out. Even for those of us who have never seen or experienced a real tornado, we see the damage that it can do. We have seen the destruction of homes, buildings, entire cities from tornados, hurricanes, tsunamis, earthquakes and violent storms. With tornadoes particularly, when we think of one, we may relate it to a monster beast. Consistent motion, violent movement, and crushing force – a chaotic scene. However, in the midst of this destructive force that eradicates anything in its way, is the core central point. A non-violent, controlled, and calm state. That would be the 'eye of the storm'.

We are often overwhelmed when we view ourselves in the middle of a world that is like a tornado. Everything around us is fast-paced and changing. A million moving parts and changing variables. Conflicting forces, clashing interests, and we are in the middle of it all feeling small and powerless. We might feel that we do not have any control over our rapidly changing surroundings. However, even if everything around us is changing, we can be the constant. We have control over ourselves. We have control over our own ideas, our decision, and our actions. We have the free will to steer our ship in any direction we desire. Each and every one of us is capable, powerful, and great because we have the ability to choose. We choose the direction we take. We own our fate through the diligence we put forth and the paths we stride. If we realize that power within, we can move mountains – no matter how young or old – we can be remarkable. Because that is what our real potential is. We are made to be remarkable. To believe in ourselves, our cause, our calling, and to dive deep into it. Just like Qassim. Go forward with your principle and don't look back. Be in the eye of the storm.

Qassim was that constant that remained in the eye of the storm when everything around him was in chaos. He witnessed soldiers being killed one after the other. He would look on as the warriors of his uncle would fall from the strikes of their enemies, staining the sands of Karbala with their noble blood. Qassim saw it all. Still, he marched forward. He knew who he was. He knew his purpose. Seeing the fierceness of the enemies, Qassim was not intimidated. He did not crumble. He did not surrender to the enemy, be it an Umayyad soldier or be it fear. He remained strong and focused, with his eyes on Imam Hussain, remembering his duty and honor before God. Qassim took control and did not allow for the brutality that he witnessed to faze him. With unparalleled valor, Qassim stood in the middle of the battlefield and let the world know who he was.

DON'T BE SOMEONE ELSE'S COPY

Hamza had a childhood friend named Abdallah. Hamza spent considerable time with Abdallah hanging out and doing the fun things all kids do. Within about a year or so in their friendship, Hamza started doing almost everything like Abdallah. The good and the bad. On one Saturday evening, Hamza was sitting at the dinner table with his family. His brother asked him a question. "How was the basketball game at the park earlier today? I couldn't make it, were there a lot of people there?" Hamza replied, "It was sick! Man you really missed out cuz! You should've seen..." His brother quickly interrupted and said, "Why do you sound like Abdallah?" Hamza sharply replied, "I don't sound like Abdallah. What do you mean I sound like Abdallah?"

"I do not hear you speaking, I hear Abdallah... You sound just like him. Literally if I were to close my eyes and hear you talk right now I would think Abdallah is having dinner. I don't remember inviting Abdallah over for dinner, do you mom?" The boys' mom held her chuckle and said, "Be nice!" Hamza was really upset and offended by his brother's remark. At the time, he did not think too much about his brother's words. But as time passed he gradually stopped hanging around Abdallah. The less he went out with Abdallah, the less his brother would point out his generic behavior. "I think Hamza's back," his brother said a few months later. Hamza finally realized that he really was acting like Abdallah and his brother's words did have merit.

If we want to be real, we have to be ourselves. That might sound obvious, but it does speak to a very important truth. In a society that is considerably open and public, we are bombarded by our exposure to other people's private and public lives, especially on television and social media. Whether it is looking at pictures of friends on Instagram, following the page of a celebrity on Facebook, or watching a reality show on TV, we become obsessed about others. We follow what *they* are doing and begin to neglect what *we* are doing, thinking, and feeling. We fixate on the new status updates of our friends and even complete strangers. Without realizing it, we subconsciously concede to their lifestyles, outlooks, and behavior. This unmonitored exposure can slowly deteriorate our foundation of principles and values. Not only that, but we begin to imitate people and lose any sense of originality we might have had or could have. Thinking that "I'm being me," we're really just subconsciously imitating the actor, singer, athlete we are following on Facebook. Or we could be picking up the tendencies, attitudes, and behaviors of our friends from school, our neighborhood, or work. We dispense of our originality and become carbon copies of others. We might not characterize it as such but in essence, we become fake.

We are all prone to falling into this because we have a tendency to want to fit in. This is even more evident when we are younger. None of us want to be loners or outsiders. We want to be popular with our family and friends. But we have to realize that if we make our self-worth contingent on the acceptance of others, we will never achieve it because it really is impossible. In fact, Imam Ali tells us, "Pleasing people is a goal that cannot be attained." People are always changing and social norms follow. Additionally, when we live in conformity just to be accepted, we lose our originality and compromise our principles and values because more frequently than not, what others are doing or what is considered to be popular or even 'normal', may be outright wrong.

Don't be someone else's photocopy. And if you can't resist copying someone, then copy someone worthwhile. Someone great. Be a photocopy of someone like Imam Hussain because when you are emulating Imam Hussain, you are developing you as you, not anyone else. Essentially, when you follow the right people and seek to emulate them, their way of life encourages you to be sincere, genuine, and original. Like his father Imam Ali said, "...Within you lies the greater universe." He doesn't confine us. He liberates us to be the greatest we can possibly be. He motivates us to be real to ourselves, to tap into our unlimited potential, and truly live our lives to the fullest. What becomes the guiding compass in our life is not the acceptance of others but alternatively true principles and values.

BEING A FORCE OF GOOD

Living with principles and values imposes many responsibilities on us. When we think of our religious responsibilities, we traditionally think of prayers, fasting, charity, etc. What about how we treat one another? What about our social interactions and conduct? What about being a force of good? Sometimes we forget that beyond the necessary rituals that are key for our spiritual growth and moral wellbeing, there is a great deal of emphasis in our faith on our ethics. The Holy Prophet said, "I was sent to perfect the best of ethics." In our ethics we have a fundamental principle, and obligation, it's called –"enjoining in good and forbidding evil". That sounds like a mouthful. So what does it mean?

Simply put, "enjoining in good" means that you promote virtue or when you see something good you encourage it. For example, if it is time to pray, you get up and encourage your friends to join you so you guys can pray together. Another example is when you see a child helping her mother, you praise her actions and offer positive reinforcement to encourage the child on sustaining such good deeds. On the other hand, "forbidding evil" is taking a stand against something bad that you witness. This can be in various forms based on the situation and surrounding circumstances. If you can lawfully stop the wrong or prevent it, that is desirable. But if that is not feasible, you might condemn it or discourage it.

The key to fulfilling this responsibility is practicing what you preach. You can't tell your friends to file their taxes when the IRS is after your business. You can't tell your sister to stop gossiping about your friend when you have a rap sheet on every other person in town. You can't tell your son to be home by 11pm when you're out with your buddies until

2am while your wife is home alone. Technically, you can say all of these things. But, you won't be effective. In fact, you would be a hypocrite. The key to enjoining in good and forbidding evil is practicing what you preach. Most of the time it is even more effective to just do what you should be doing, modeling behavior for others, rather than lecturing others on what they ought to do. "Call onto our path without your tongues." – Imam Ja'far Al-Sadiq.

PRINCIPLE VERSUS PREFERENCE

One essential concept to keep in mind when it comes to "enjoining in good, and forbidding evil" is separating between principles and preferences. A principle is a fundamental truth that must not be compromised or negotiated. Principles are objective, they should not be held or assessed on arbitrary standards. When we begin to assess or apply principles arbitrarily we offend the integrity of the principle and defy the entire purpose of what a principle is there for. Principles are meant to be constants in our lives, things we should not deviate from because they are key to our success and happiness. Just like our principles, we have to be constant and objective in observing them and applying them. Think of the principles and values you live by: justice, honesty, integrity, modesty, equality, etc. If you bend on the things you consider principles, you're not treating them the way you should.

On to preferences. A preference is a liking, a fondness, a taste for one thing over another. Some people like orange juice and others like apple juice. And some people don't like either. Weird. We love juice. Unlike a principle, preferences are arbitrary. It is imperative to distinguish between the two and not mix them because each requires a different course of conduct and behavior. While it is important to be flexible and open to different perspectives and insights, disputes on principles require firm resolve and steadfastness. Remember principles are not like juice. When we are talking about preferences, however, we should be more flexible and open to others' ideas. At the end of the day, as much as individuals should define themselves by their principles, their preferences tend to make up a great deal of that identity as well. There is no right and wrong when it comes to a preference, unless the preference is in conflict with a principle. Then, the principle always wins.

Now, let's explore this issue in the Holy Quran. God states, "And from among you should be a party that should invite to good and enjoin in what is right and forbid the wrong, and those are the ones that are successful."[29] In order to be one that enjoins in the good and forbids the evil, you have to make your vital decisions based on principle and not preference. In a likely situation where your preference might conflict with the principle, the principle must override the preference.

Why do we say the things we say? Why do we dress the way we dress? Who are our friends and why do we hang out with them? Where do we spend our time and why? Take Billy for example. Billy gets up in the morning, checks his Facebook and messages his friends. He gets dressed, puts on his favorite muscle shirt, his dark blue jeans, sprays some Axe and leaves the house. Billy is pretty honest. When we ask him why do you dress like that, he says, "Girls like it. I do it for them." Principle or preference here? Contrary to some pretty fit people out there, wearing a muscle shirt is not a principle. And given the implication, Billy's preference is in conflict with some principles – modesty, bashfulness, respect of the opposite sex, etc. Whether it's at home or outside, no matter where we are going, we need to ask ourselves an essential question: why am I doing this? If it is based on a principle, excellent. If it based on a preference, we need to make sure that preference is not in conflict with any of our principles. The way we walk, talk, interact with others; is that based on a

---

[29] The Holy Quran, 3:104.

principle or a preference? If we find ourselves to be providing disappointing answers, that's fine. The first step to improvement is identifying the problem. Ask yourself questions. Reflect. Answer and be honest with yourself. Try to do the right thing. Remind yourself that you are a principled person and you're bigger than a desire, a whim, or a baseless drive to 'feel good'. You're bigger than that. When you fall, pick yourself back up and try again. Don't give up. If you do, you'll just be stuck in the mundane routines of life and carry on with unfavorable habits and a lifestyle that you'll look back on and wished you changed.

And let's be frank. Being principled and living principally is not easy. It is pretty hard. When you find yourself sitting in a car with a bunch of friends, music blasting, and they start passing around something that looks like a cigarette, what do you do? It might be difficult for you to challenge your friends and tell them to lower the music, let alone tell them to stop smoking. You don't want to be left out or looked at in a weird way by your friends. No one wants to be a 'party-pooper'. We've all been in situations like that before, and at times, failed to stand our ground and be an advocate for our principles. But if you can't be an advocate for what you believe in then at least don't be a participant in something you don't.

HOW TO BE A FORCE OF GOOD

The Prophet's family always emphasized the importance of the type of approach we have with people we interact with. Imam Al-Sadiq instructs us on the various qualities that a person who enjoins what is good ought to have. These qualities are prerequisites for those of us who want to enjoin in good, the right way. These requirements are necessary ingredients for our success in being a force of good. The Imam says that the first quality is that the person must be "knowledgeable about what is permissible and what is forbidden." There is a famous Arab proverb that says, "One who doesn't have something, cannot give it." If I do not know halal from haram, right from wrong, appropriate from inappropriate, how will I be able to teach and guide others? We have to start with ourselves first and foremost. Learning the principles and applying them in our lives. As we advance in our self-development, we can also help others along the way. But the key remains starting with ourselves and equipping ourselves with knowledge.

The Imam continues, "He must be free from his personal inclinations regarding what he enjoins and forbids, give good counsel to people, be merciful and compassionate to them, and call them with gentleness in a very clear manner, while recognizing their different characters so that he can put each in his proper place." These statements encompass many lessons, but they all speak to the approach that we should have when we wish to teach or guide others. Some narrow minded, often confused, people understand enjoining in good and forbidding evil as going around and calling people out on everything wrong they do. *Halal! Haram!* Right! Wrong! That is not what Imam Al-Sadiq is prescribing in this narration.

The Imam is teaching us that, not only do we need to have the knowledge and content, we need to have the right approach. An approach of a counselor not a judge. An approach with mercy and compassion not intolerance and harshness. An approach that is uplifting not degrading. An approach that takes into account the other person's sensitivities, knowledge, and maturity, so that the message is tailored for that person. Most importantly in all of this is that we lead by example and realize that we are not judges. God is the one and only judge. None of us have been assigned by God to send people to hell or heaven. That is not our job. Our job is to help each grow and be there for one other. Treat others the way you would like to be treated. We heard this all the time as kids. It would be a good idea to actually use it as adults.

HAND, SPEECH, AND HEART

There are different ways to enjoin in good and forbid evil. Imam Ali explains the three different forms by classifying them into degrees of priority. To better understand the different degrees and how they interplay, we will use a scenario throughout. Two friends, Khalil and Mustafa, meet their classmates to play street basketball at the local park. Fifteen minutes into the game, after aggressive and intense play from both teams, Mustafa and an opposing player get into a verbal argument that quickly escalates into a physical altercation.

The highest degree and most effective way is with your hand, meaning to take physical action. In our scenario, Khalil intervenes to break up the fight, grabs Mustafa by the arm and pulls him to leave the park and go back home. Here, Khalil physically intervened, took action to end the fight, and removed Mustafa from the premises altogether. If Khalil is not physically able to break the fight due to some type of limitation, the next degree of forbidding evil would be speech. Khalil would try to talk Mustafa out of fighting and try to persuade him to leave in order to stay out of trouble. He would also attempt to talk to the other person and try to calm things down with his words.

However, if Khalil does that to no avail and no one is listening, the third degree is to condemn this action in his heart. In this case, if Khalil is not able to break the fight himself or talk the guys out of fighting, he might leave the premises altogether and call 911 for help. Khalil would not stay on the court because he does not approve of what is occurring and his leave is a message of disapproval of what is taking place. To summarize the three degrees, the Imam states that a person should enjoin in good and forbid evil first with his hand. If he is unable to do that, then he should do so with his speech. If he cannot be effective through his speech, then he must at least be against the wrong that is done in his heart. A person must be considerate and aware of the situation and the circumstances before he takes any course of action.

PROTECTING THE FAITH

It is important not to lose sight of why we have to enjoin in good and forbid evil. Remember it is not about being a police officer that issues a ticket every time someone commits a 'sharia violation' or a judge who recites a verdict and sentences people to hellfire. It is about the collective consciousness to do good and refrain from wrong so that we can live better lives both in this life and the hereafter. It is about helping one another through educating ourselves on our rights and responsibilities, leading by example, and promoting good. The Prophet is narrated to have said, "Enjoining the good and forbidding the evil is the way of the prophets and path of the scholars. It is a tremendous obligation through which (other) obligatory tasks are undertaken and religious creeds are safeguarded."

This puts in perspective why Imam Hussain led his epic revolution sacrificing his life. He was facing a tyrant that wanted to kill Islam by distorting it. A misguided ruler that wanted to undermine the religion by distorting its creed and principles. Yazid became his own legislator and was willing to enact whatever policy he needed to advance his own personal political agenda. The message of Islam that the Prophet successfully brought forth was going to be compromised. Imam Hussain had to take action to preserve the faith and safeguard the creed. This is his legacy that Hussain left behind. "I do not revolt due to discontent, nor out of arrogance. I did not rise as a corruptor, nor as an oppressor. Rather, I wish to call for reform in the nation of my grandfather. I wish to call for what is good, and to forbid what is evil."

Imam Hussain awakened people. The corruption and oppression was widespread and people witnessed it, but they did not challenge it. They accepted it, even if it was only implicitly. Today where do we stand when we see wrong? Do we just brush it under the carpet? Do we turn a blind eye? What is our position on what happens around us? We're not talking about judging others or being condescending. Absolutely not. Being judgmental and condescending is a whole different beast in itself. Like we mentioned previously, check yourself before you look to check others. The first challenge lies within. We have to be real to ourselves before we wish to be a source of guidance for others.

Nine

Be the Change

Starting with the Change Within

"If the religion of Muhammad will not remain intact except by my death, then o' swords take me." That popularized line of poetry manifested the spirit of Imam Hussain's revolution. He did not seek death, he sought life. He sought life for Islam, even if it meant sacrificing everything he had. The Imam faced a point of time when Islam was on the brink of collapse. Its ethics, laws, and identity were being threatened by the rise of political rulers who used the name of Islam for their own material gains. The spirit of the nation was dead. It had fallen into a deep coma. To reawaken it required a shock, a shock so severe that nations a thousand years later would still feel it. The sacrifice and tragedy of Imam Hussain was that shock that reawakened the nation. He was the change that he wanted to see in the world. In our time, it is no different. If you want to see change in the world, you have to be that change. Be the change you want to see.

Most things around us might be out of our control. However, the one constant we definitely have control over is ourselves. We have full and exclusive authority over ourselves. We can control what we say, what we do, the thoughts and ideas we adopt, and the principles we live by. To be effective forces of change in our communities, we need to start by instilling that change within. God addresses this in the Holy Quran. He says, "God will not change the condition of a people until they change what is in themselves."[30] The change and progress of a community starts with the change and progress of the individuals.

Even if we don't have influence over other people, we have control over ourselves. Each and every one of us is in control. Imagine if we all decided to change ourselves for the better, as individuals. That would naturally follow to a collective change, because we are all doing it. Imagine that. We can make a world of a change. We just have to do it ourselves. We should never be complacent. We should always strive to advance as individuals by pursuing knowledge, expanding our horizons, and enriching our experiences. Doing that effectively comes with consistent reflection and self-assessment. If we find ourselves falling off course, we need pull it together and get back on track. Don't beat yourself up if you fall off, just refocus and keep moving forward. We have all gone through our fair share of ups and downs – we still do – but don't let those dips keep you down too long. Remind yourself of your great purpose and stay the course. Remember, what you do on your journey is just as important as where you're going.

---

[30] The Holy Quran, 13:11.

BEING COMPASSIONATE

To be a force of positive change, one ought to reach out to others. We have to be the extending hand, starting with our close circle of family and friends and extending outwards to others such as colleagues, community members, etc. Human beings are naturally social beings. Even for introverts, people generally don't like to live in complete isolation. We live and thrive in groups. We long for company, even if it is the company of a loved one, a dear friend, or a partner. Civilizations were built with groups of people coming together and finding common social norms to live by. We all have a social responsibility to one another. Only when we work as a collective for the social good, can we advance as communities and societies. So how do we effectively reach out to others and move in that direction?

One day an elderly Meccan woman decided to go shopping in the local market. She had quite an appetite and bought a little too much for her to handle. Holding bags filled with fruits, vegetables, wheat, meat, spices, and knickknacks she had bargained for, she could barely walk straight. Seeing her struggling to leave the market, a young man quickly approached her. The young man stood tall, handsome, and confident. She hadn't seen many like him. "Can I help you with your bags?" He asked with a smile. "Oh, thank you my dear! Of course! Thank you!" She was elated and relieved. The young man held her groceries effortlessly and walked her home. As they walked along the dirt road that led to her house, she felt comfortable enough to speak her mind to this young man she just met. "My dear, thank you so much for your help. You have really been so kind. I have a piece of advice for you, please keep it near and dear." The young man continued to smile politely as she spoke. "There is a man named Muhammad. Stay away from him. His family and tribe once knew him to be honest and trustworthy, but now he is bringing an absurd claim that there is only one God!" The young man continued to listen attentively. "Because of him there is no peace. Because of him we're all troubled. He is misleading people! The poor, the weak, the slaves think they've found freedom by following him. Even the youth have become corrupted by his twisted brand of truth!" They were nearing the old woman's house now. "Thank you my dear young man! I've talked so much I barely felt the time pass." He responded with his beaming smile. "But my dear, you've helped me all this way and I didn't have the manners to ask you where you're from. Forgive me for being so rude. What is your name dear?" He smiled and said, "Muhammad."

We need that kind of compassion. The compassion of the Prophet who gave only a kind smile to even those who wished him harm. We need that sort of compassion in our hearts to reach out to others, near and far. What would we have done if we were in the Prophet's place? Imagine helping someone and they began bashing you, not knowing who you were. Most of us would drop the lady's bags and say, "See ya!" But that's not how the Prophet was. He knew his purpose was greater than being affected by people's immaturity, lack of understanding, or ignorance. With a simple smile the Prophet was able to change that woman's entire perspective on him and the faith. He not only changed her perspective, she converted to the faith and became a devout believer in God. Imagine the power of that smile. That smile changed a person's life. In fact, it changed countless lives.

Imam Hussain had that same compassion. Until the last moments before the battle ensued, Imam Hussain reached out to his opponents and invited them to the straight path. He called on them with mercy and compassion to change their ways but to no avail. They were adamant on killing him and his companions. To the few that did leave the Umayyad camp, like Hur Al-Riyahi, the Imam welcomed them and forgave them. Hur, in particular, was the general who prevented Imam Hussain's caravan from reaching Kufa and stopped them in Karbala. On the day of Ashura and before the battle commenced, Hur was found pacing back and forth outside his tent.

Some of the Umayyad soldiers came to him and asked him, "Hur are you okay? You look yellow in the face. We know you to be one of the bravest warriors..." Hur replied, "I am choosing between heaven and hell..." As Hur paused and the soldiers looked at each other confused, he made his decision. "And I can't choose anything over heaven..." Hur jumped on his horse and rode to the camp of Imam Hussain. Upon reaching the camp, he got down from his horse and kneeled before the Imam begging him for forgiveness. "Is there repentance for me, my master?" Imam Hussain accepted his repentance and prayed for him. It is narrated that the Imam said, "Your mother named you well Hur." Hur means *free*.

We are all moved when we remember these stories of mercy, compassion, and love. We should measure our own compassion against that of the Prophet and the Imams. Of course we will fall short. But when we put it in perspective, at least we know if we are in the right direction.

Compassion starts at home. We need to love and respect our family all the time. Not just some of the time, but every day. Respecting our parents. Appreciating our spouses. Being kind to our siblings. Showing mercy to our kids. Reaching out to our relatives. Taking all of these people in our hearts and treating them with the compassion of Prophet Muhammad and Imam Hussain. Don't you think that is a sure step for a happier life? Try it and see.

We have all been mistreated in one way or another. It could have been by a friend, family member, or even a stranger. It doesn't feel good. No one wants to be looked down upon. So naturally, we respond with anger, spite, and even reciprocate the mistreatment. But what if we misunderstood the person mistreating us? What if they truly didn't mean it? What if they are going through their own issues themselves? "Well that's not my problem," you may say. True. It isn't. But wouldn't you want people to be considerate of you when you are having an off day? We all need a pass once in a while.

Put yourself in the other person's shoes. Your father might have had a rough day at work and so he raised his voice when you asked him for a new phone. Your sister might be anxious about her exam and so she kicked you out of her room because you were being annoying. Your boss might be stressed out about the plummeting business of the company and so he dismissed your questions during the meeting. Your father, sister, boss, or anyone else are not necessarily disrespecting or mistreating you deliberately. Their own problems are seeping into the rest of their lives and it happened to affect you. Now, you're in the right to feel upset. These conditions don't excuse behavior. But, instead of adding fuel to the fire and making the problem bigger than it should be, be the rock. Be solid, calm, and polite. Be the compassionate one. Be the better person, and they will realize it and appreciate you for it.

BEING THE INITIATOR

One of the key qualities in a successful person is being proactive. Most personal development books speak to this principle. We have to initiate compassion. We have to initiate good behavior and lead by example. A lot of times, relationships fail because we fail at communication. In other words, we fail to initiate communication. Why? They didn't call me or text me, so why should I call or text them? Both sides holds out in that sense and no one talks for months. Friendships are shattered, families are broken, and marriages are ruined because of this simple issue. The other side drops the ball and we feel we need to do the same. Kamal's brother Alexander lives in New York, while Kamal lives in Michigan. Alexander doesn't call Kamal for several months. Kamal thinks to himself, "He hasn't found the time to call me. I don't have the time to call him." Kamal is right to be upset, but what if something happened to his brother? Even if he is in perfect health, Kamal should be the bigger person. Instead of waiting for your brother to call you, be the initiator. Pick up the phone or shoot him a quick text message. Like mom says, "Call your brother!"

One of our mentors gave us a piece of advice a while back. He told us, "Don't wait for people to do good to you before you do good to them... you will only set yourself up for disappointment, and it is always best to be the initiator. Start with good and good will be done to you, if not by them then surely by Him." Initiating good really does go a long way with people. Even people that might not be too fond of you will eventually be impressed by your good character. Your consistency in good conduct will change their attitude towards you. Again, it is important to make it clear that we are not saying you should let people step all over you. By all means, do not be a doormat. The Prophet and the Imams all emphasized the importance of an individual's honor and dignity, so much so that it was said that a believer's life is more sacred than the Ka'ba itself. Without compromising our dignity, if there is an opportunity for us to build bridges or make mends with people, we should absolutely go for it.

Maintaining this spirit of initiating good requires that we be willing to forgive. Practically, we need to let some things slide. Not everything has to turn into a debate about right and wrong. You will exhaust yourself and the people around you. Pick your battles. When the Prophet was hurt by his people, he didn't call them out every time they did something wrong. He was a mercy to them. He forgave them. Of course, he did reprimand when needed but that wasn't what he did all the time. He taught his people by his example. So, let's not turn small stuff into big stuff.

We cannot become consumed in anger and hurt every time something bad happens to us. "*Woe is me!*" – that shouldn't be *you*. In our crazy fast-paced world we deal with so many people in various capacities every day. People will do things, intentionally or unintentionally, that will tick us off, hurt us, or even embarrass us. Your classmate always asks the most random questions and takes up from lecture time. Your friend hasn't called you in months and when you texted them all they said was, "Sorry. I'm busy." Your colleague undermines you in a work meeting in front of a client. These are all things that will anger us, upset us or just down right annoy us. It's up to us on how we handle these situations and these feelings. Do we get infuriated and allow these small things to ruin our day and steal our joy? Or do we let certain things slide and move on to more important things in our lives? We have to make these decisions every day.

FORGIVE SO THAT YOU CAN BE FORGIVEN

Every day, we make mistakes and commit sins. Just count all the times you hurt the people you love. Your mother, your father, your friends, your colleagues. How many times have you delayed your prayers or even ignored praying altogether? How many times have you seen the wrong in what you were about to do, and still did it anyway? We know ourselves. It has been just too many times. No one knows you better than you, and God. So do we give up? Not at all. Because holding on to Him gives us hope. We can never despair in God's mercy. No matter where we are in life, no matter what mistakes we've made, and no matter how far off track we've gone... God is always there. He isn't going anywhere.

God's doors are open to us if we want to enter. We don't even have to knock, we just need to walk through. If God's doors are always open to us, shouldn't we keep our doors open to each other? Not literally of course. You should shut the front door to your house and lock it behind you. Safety first. Shouldn't we be considerate and willing to forgive others that have wronged us? You might say, "This person doesn't deserve my forgiveness." We ask you, do you really believe any of us are deserving of God's forgiveness? After all that God has given us, and after all that we have done in return, do you think we're in a position to expect God's mercy because of our merit? Of course not. However, that doesn't deter us from seeking it because we understand that God's mercy is all-encompassing. His forgiveness moves us forward. His love keeps us alive.

Life is too short to hold grudges and be bitter. It's a waste of time, energy, and even money at times. People can get crazy when they're bitter. There are bigger and more important things in life than to blacklist your friends for hurting your feelings. Whether its big or small, intentional or unintentional, we should try our best to give people second chances. Just think about how many chances God gives us every single day.

GIVE PEOPLE THE BENEFIT OF THE DOUBT

One of the reasons why relationships become strained and yesterday's friends becomes today's foes is that we do not give people the benefit of the doubt. Imam Ali addresses this issue head on. He instructs us, "Give your brother seventy excuses." Yes, seventy excuses. We mentioned it before and we mention it again. This is something that we need to pay attention to because neglecting this really can be devastating. People's reputations have been ruined because people in the community decided to jump to the worst conclusions. Let's not even go as far as giving seventy excuses. Let's at least afford people a few, or even just one excuse at the minimum. We should be considerate enough to give people the benefit of the doubt. We owe it to each other.

Your uncle invites you to a big family reunion. You intend on going but on that day of, an emergency project comes up at work and you have to work overtime to meet the deadline. Story of our lives. You are so overwhelmed by your work, you forget to show up or even communicate an apology. The next day, you hear from your brother that your uncle is very upset and disappointed. He complained to your father saying, "Your son is so inconsiderate. I don't get it. He doesn't show up and he doesn't call! Does he think his friends or his work are more important that family? This is not right, not at all." You love your uncle. In fact, you have a great relationship with him. So when you hear that from your brother you're pretty hurt.

You were really looking forward to the family reunion. You actually went out of your way the week before to clear your schedule so you can make it. You have every right to feel upset and hurt by your uncle's comments. You had the best of intentions but life happens. Work happens. How nice would it have been if, instead of jumping to conclusions, your uncle called to check up on you to see if everything was okay. Yeah, that would have been great. But think to yourself, how many times have you done the same thing your uncle did to your friends and family. We've all been that uncle. Don't be that uncle. He's a great guy but in this regard he's not that amicable. Each and every one of us needs to change that in ourselves. The next time someone does something that bothers you, take a deep breath and recall Imam Ali's advice. Give people the benefit of the doubt so that they can give you the benefit of the doubt.

SERVING THE COMMUNITY

To be a catalyst of positive change, not only do you need to strive to reach out to others, you need to reach out with a purpose to serve others. We all have a greater social responsibility to serve the community. If we do not extend our hands to help the community and be part of it, we are not going to see the real significance in ourselves as individuals. We can all do well for ourselves and our families. Obtain a good education, have a successful career, make a lot of money and buy all the toys we desire. However, if that is all we do, our success will be confined to us as individuals. But if we do all of that for ourselves and our families and at the same time bring other people with us along the way, that success has broadened its reach. Those people can be our family members, our colleagues, friends, and our community members. At that point, our life becomes more purposeful because we become part of something bigger than just ourselves. We become part of a larger community.

MAKE SERVICE AN INTEGRAL PART OF LIFE

To be part of that larger community, you must make service an integral part of your life. Moreover, that service has to be unconditional and without an expectation for something in return. There is a beautiful story in the Holy Quran that puts all of this in perspective. God states in the Holy Quran, "And they give food out of love for Him to the poor and the orphan and the captive. We only feed you for God's sake; we desire from you neither reward nor thanks."[31]

One day Imam Ali and his family were fasting. Like usual, they planned to break their fast with a very simple meal, usually nothing more than bread and water. As they were preparing to break their fast after sunset, a poor man knocked on their door and asked for food. The Imam gave their dinner to the poor man and remained fasting for another day. On the second day, once again as they were preparing to break their fast, an orphan knocked on the door. The orphan asked for food and water. Without hesita-

---

[31] The Holy Quran, 76:8.

tion, they offered the little food they had to the orphan. Their unbroken fast continued for a third day. At sunset, a prisoner knocked on the door and they happily gave their food away again. God revealed the verse above in their honor. God adds that they offered this charity to those people, not seeking reward or thanks from them, but rather for the sake of His sake alone.

There is much to be taken away from this story. First, we have to make it part of who we are to give and offer when we can. We do not have to fast for three days, but really look at the inspiration that this Holy Household give us. Three days. Without food or water. Out of choice. That required an unmatched rock solid will and patience. We don't have to go that far, but we can do a lot. It can be as simple as offering some of your food to those around you before you eat. Have a sense of generosity that our religion and culture promote.

Steve was returning on an early flight from Kansas City, Missouri. He got on the plane and sat in his designated seat. An older women was already sitting in the seat next to him. Right before the flight took off, she took out a sandwich from her bag. In her soft voice she said, "I'm sorry for eating in front of you. I have to take my medication and the doctor says I must eat a bite before taking this," she held up the little white pill showing it to Steve. "Would you like a piece? It's not much but we can share." Steve was taken back by her generosity. It really wasn't much, Steve could have eaten that sandwich in one bite. But the way she offered... it was just so genuine. She really wanted to give him the sandwich, and if it wasn't for the medication she would have. "Thank you so much, you really are too kind." Steve said to her smiling.

Steve didn't stop thinking about her offering for the entirety of the plane ride. Before he got home, he stopped at the local drug store to buy some groceries and snacks. As he finished from his quick stop and walked to his car with his bags of groceries, he saw a homeless man sitting on the corner of the street. Not waiting for the homeless man to ask for anything, Steve walked up to him and gave him half of his groceries. The homeless man was confused at first and then quickly elated. "Thank you! You are too kind, thank you!" Steve went back home and his wife asked him, "Where's the rest of the stuff Steve?" He got back in his car and bought more groceries. Can't get it right all the time, can we?

One day, when Imam Ali was praying in Masjid Al-Nabawee – the Mosque of Prophet Muhammad – a poor man walked in asking for help. No one paid attention to him. Disappointed he helplessly started to make his way out. Imam Ali was in the state of *Rukoo'* in his prayer. He heard the man's call for help. Before the man left, the Imam held out his hand signaling to the man to take the Imam's ring. Understanding the Imam's signal, the poor man took the ring and jumped with joy. After the exchange, the following verse was revealed in honor of Imam Ali:

"Your guardian is only Allah, His Apostle, and the faithful who maintain the prayer and give the zakat while bowing down." The part, "Those who believe...who keep up prayers and pay the poor while they bow," refers to this historical incident when the Imam gave the destitute his ring. In this example, the Imam teaches us that offering charity is a pillar of our faith. It is such a priority that it is not bound by time or place. Whenever the opportunity is present, we should invest in it. It is an investment because our Imams tell us that charity alleviates tribulations. Consequently, a good practice to get accustomed to is to pay charity every morning before we leave the house. Even if it's just dollar or less. God willing, that charity will protect us from adversity and trouble. The reward for that charity in the hereafter is even beyond what we can imagine.

GIVE UNCONDITIONALLY FOR THE CAUSE

Giving and serving become much more meaningful when they are done unconditional for a cause. Unconditional means there are no strings attached.

Giving or serving, not expecting something in return. For example, Mary donates a significant sum of money to a humanitarian organization, not to buy influence or for notoriety, but rather because she genuinely believes in the cause. Moses volunteers several hours in a soup kitchen every Saturday not because he needs the community service hours to graduate, but because he really wants to support the needy. For all the students out there, the community service hours you receive is not unfavorable. It is a great incentive. But the point is that your intention shouldn't be exclusive to just getting hours out of it, whereby if you suddenly weren't getting your community service hours you would just quit. Serve and give selflessly. Don't do it for what you will get out of it. Do it for the honor and virtue that comes with it. No one gave as selflessly as the Imams.

It was a common practice for the Imams to go around at night and anonymously drop off food at the homes of poor families. They did nightly rounds and never revealed their identities. They did not reveal their identities because they did not desire to receive credit from people. They did it because of the virtue in the act itself. They did it because it was what God wanted. This is the best type of charity. It is not easy to have that state of mind. We generally like to be recognized. We are delighted when people commend us and give us a pat on the back. There is nothing wrong with wanting to be looked at in a favorable way, but it's different when the purpose behind your charitable acts is recognition. Striking that balance can be challenging. Nevertheless, it is something we should strive for. This is one way to better ourselves and grow... that is to give unconditionally.

THE LITTLE THINGS MATTER

Being helpful doesn't necessitate you donate millions of dollars or volunteer thousands of hours. You can be helpful and give by doing the little things. It could be something small but meaningful. Helping your aging neighbor cut his grass. Helping your aunt's son with his reading. Volunteering two to three hours every month at the mosque or local soup kitchen. All of these things might seem minor. They do not cost you money or require much time or effort. However, in the eyes of your neighbor, your aunt, and the organizers of the mosque, you are doing a great service that they recognize and appreciate. It might sound like a cliché, but with these small acts, you really are making the world a better place.

We know a person that left behind a legacy in our community by doing the little things. This person had minimal education and spent his whole life as a blue-collar worker. He lived a modest life but dedicated all his spare time serving people. He volunteered countless hours every month at the local mosques. He used his personal network to raise money throughout the year for orphaned victims of terrorism. He would continuously visit the sick and attend funerals. He was a whole organization, a whole community, embodied in one body. When he passed away, thousands of people in the community attended his funeral. Not because he was a celebrity or wealthy, but because he reserved for himself a place in people's hearts with his humility, integrity, and service.

BE PART OF A TEAM

We can all do good work by serving in our individual capacities. However, we can amplify the level of our work and maximize on our potential when we work in teams. Very early on in our community work, one of our mentors taught us a lesson that truly changed our outlook on life. He shared with us, "You can work and achieve a lot in life. But you can achieve so much more and reach unimaginable heights when you become part of a team that works collectively for one goal. When you find that team and you click with them, you will be able to move mountains." These words continued to resonate with us and has really shaped our outlook with respect to community work. We have been blessed to have found a team that we work with on so many different levels. We started as friends and colleagues, and now we are a big family. We work together, plan together, travel together, and serve together.

As our mentor taught us, when you have a harmonious team, you can move mountains. A testament to that is a project we worked on for four years with a group of bright and dedicated team members. It started as an idea floating around in a gathering that we had. We were sitting down with two other people discussing different initiatives and efforts that we can work on to serve the community. After throwing a few ideas around, we decided to pursue what, at the time, seemed to be very far-fetched. We started conducting elaborative research on the logistics, costs, market, etc. We reached out to different organizations in the community to partner with us on the initiative, sought community businesses to sponsor the costs, and commenced with planning.

The team comprised of more than 10 individuals working tirelessly over the course of 6 months to raise the money, finalize all the planning, and put all the pieces together to execute the project. What started as a simple idea tossed around between a few of us flourished into one of the most successful efforts in our community. We were 10 core individuals and an extended support team of two hundred volunteers. All of us understood that if it was not for the team spirit and the collective minds, we could not even dream of accomplishing this project. Every team member was important and brought value to the table. One person would work on the business plan. Another would raise funds. The third would recruit volunteers. The fourth would design all the artwork and marketing material. Every person was a different piece to the puzzle. When all the pieces came together, we truly moved mountains.

Become a Leader in Your Community

It is much easier to just go with the flow and be a follower. It is much more difficult to lead. Leading does not mean to pursue power, exert influence over others, or command people. True leaders are the ones that can create positive change in their environments by identifying problems and finding solutions. Successful leaders are ones that can rally and organize people to work for a common cause. Leaders think long-term and work within a strategy. They do not seek temporary results only. They are in it for the long run. They are progressive, humble, and are the first ones to pull up their sleeves and get their hands dirty.

Every community has its problems. Many of the problems are common and some are unique. Whether it is poverty, inadequate education, lack of civic participation, or something else, we are responsible for making a change. Each and every one of us can be a leader in one way or another. We must all aspire to become leaders in our communities by developing our skills and utilizing them to serve the advancement of our communities. It can be large scale or small scale. That depends on various factors such as the dynamic of the community, resources, opportunities, politics, etc. Regardless of what the specific conditions are, we can all strive to lead efforts that can improve the condition of our community.

It can be leading an effort with the neighbors to clean the local neighborhood park so that it is safe and sanitary for the kids to play in. Alternatively, it can be establishing a youth group at the local mosque to organize year round programs to serve the youth attendees. Another effort could be launching a campaign that mobilizes people to go to the polls on Election Day. These are all different ideas that might be helpful in many communities. You might have a creative idea for a new initiative that you are passionate about. Go for it. Make it happen. As long as your intention is pure, the will is there, and there is good work ethic, you can become a leader and a catalyst of effective change in your community.

Ten

Be
Extraordinary

YOUR POTENTIAL IS LIMITLESS

Imam Hussain and his seventy-two companions went up against thirty thousand Umayyad soldiers on the day of Ashura. They fought until their very last breath. They were all martyred. Their legacy lives and their story has resonated over the past 1,400 years with millions of people. Today, millions upon millions remember their story, revere their characters, and take them as examples. How can such a small group of individuals have such an impact? Each and every one of the seventy-two knew his potential was limitless. They knew that they were on the path of greatness. They knew they were extraordinary.

Imam Hussain didn't reserve being extraordinary for himself. He inspired his companions and followers to be the same. He inspired everyone with him to be devout believers in God, servants of their community, and defenders of justice and truth. You have the likes of John the Servant, Hur Al-Riyahi, Habib ibn Muthaher, Zuhayr ibn Al-Qayn, and the list goes on. These individuals were not immaculate or from the Holy Household. Yet, they were extraordinary because they chose to be through their creed and their actions. Just like them, we can be great too. All of us, wherever we are at, can also be extraordinary if we choose to be.

We all aspire to lead positive lives and become successful individuals. But what separates those who dream and those who actually achieve their dreams? Successful people believe in themselves and their potential. They live their lives with a mindset that they are capable. They will put in the time, work hard, progress, and accomplish their goals. No matter what the obstacles are, they have the resilience and willpower to triumph. No matter how hard it may get, they know deep down how strong they are and that in the end they will persevere.

DON'T UNDERMINE YOURSELF

We are our biggest obstacles. We hold ourselves down through our needless worries and negativity. We can't expect to be successful in life when we are constantly undermining our abilities and looking for every defect in ourselves. Self-evaluation and introspection are great, but there is a fine line between them and destructively criticizing ourselves. This is a recipe for failure, misery, and regression. We are our biggest critics.

Sara is so consumed with her looks. Before she steps out of the house, she spends hours looking into the mirror wondering whether she is beautiful or not. Wondering whether she needs to put on more make up, change her outfit, or even leave the house altogether... She thinks about it so much it hurts. Insecure, hesitant, distressed, she doesn't know what to do. To Sara we say, you are beautiful. But you're more beautiful when you are confident. You are more beautiful when you are grateful. You are more beautiful when stop worrying about if other people think you're beautiful. You're even more beautiful when you're more concerned with your ideas rather than your looks. Because you're better than that. You're more than that. And you should want more for yourself. Don't give yourself the short end of the stick. Beauty fades, your character stays forever.

We shouldn't underestimate ourselves, because when we do we are undermining the status that God has given each and every one of us. In every prayer we perform, we repeat the statement, *Allahu Akbar*, God is Great. God is great in every way, shape, and form. He is not limited or confined. He is infinite. Thus, if we connect to Him and hold on to His rope, we should never despair or feel any sense of limitation. Our strength, power, and ability come from Him. But we have to really believe in that. Wake up every morning and remember that He is there for you. He is watching over you, protecting you, and guiding your path. He wants you to be successful, happy, and extraordinary. He wants great things for you. Hold on to Him. Don't let go.

We need to stop shackling ourselves and burying our heads in the sand. And it all starts by truly believing in our potential as individuals, groups, and communities. When we realize our potential, we will move mountains. Although we all have unending potential, we naturally have different abilities and talents. The first step is for each and every one of us to reflect and dig deep to find that potential. This does not happen in one or two hours. It's a journey that takes time, effort, and willingness to experience and learn. We need to be willing to learn, experiment, and try different things until we can pinpoint exactly where that true potential is.

The Imams teach us that each and every one of us should aspire to be the best we can be in anything we do. If you want to become an engineer, aspire to receive the best education possible so you can become the top professional in your field. If you decide you want to pursue innovation, aspire to create the next revolutionary product and make it the best in the business. If you set your mind to become a writer, make it your goal to write the next international best-seller. All of these goals and ambitions are reasonable and legitimate. Our dreams can become reality. We just have to hold on to His rope and believe in ourselves.

CONFIDENCE VERSUS ARROGANCE

Our religion is about balance and moderation. We should never take extremes because extremism is the recipe to failure. As much as we stressed the vitality of believing in one's potential and having self-confidence, we have to be cautious of our confidence turning into arrogance. There is a day-and-night distinction between these two. Self-confidence is to have a sense of belief and assurance in your personal power and ability. This is a virtue we should all develop in ourselves. On the contrary, arrogance is to feel that you are better or superior to others. That is problematic because as God states in the Holy Quran, the only measurement for superiority in the eyes of God is piety. Not race, ethnicity, wealth, education, but rather righteousness and virtue.

Sam was a bright and intelligent guy with a great personality. He took care of his parents, excelled in his schooling, and generously volunteered his time to serve the community. He went to medical school and became a successful doctor. However, it didn't take much time to notice that there was a change in his attitude and conduct. His parents complained that he rarely visited them and when he did, he did not show the respect and appreciation they were used to. He became disconnected from the community and dropped his childhood friends.

After being disconnected from him for about three years, his old friend Abraham came across him at a community event. Abraham was really happy to see Sam and catch up. Sam wasn't shy to express his mind. He started to undermine his family and bash the community. He told Abe, "The last several years of school and work have taught me that I need to climb out of the cave I've been living in my whole life. These people are backwards, unsophisticated, and good for nothing... I am too good to waste my precious time with these people." Abe was absolutely stunned. He knew the guy became disconnected from his hometown, but he didn't expect anything like that. Abe was speechless. Sam had accomplished so much in his life as a bright student and rising professional. But that didn't justify his arrogance. For him to think that the family and community that raised him are 'backwards' and that he is 'too good' for them was beyond foolish. It was down right disgusting. There's no room for that in faith, culture, or humanity. If you're arrogant go find another table to sit. "I wonder at the arrogant man who was just a drop of semen the other day and will turn into a corpse tomorrow." – Imam Ali. So tell us again, what are you arrogant about?

LOOK FOR EXTRAORDINARY IN ORDINARY

A reporter approached two workers, Jamal and Youssef. The reporter asked Jamal, "What are you doing?" Jamal responded, "I am virtually a slave, an underpaid bricklayer who spends his days wasting his time, placing bricks on top of one another." The reporter asked Youssef the same question. Youssef replied, "I'm the luckiest person in the world. I get to be part of important and beautiful pieces of architecture. I help turn simple pieces of brick into exquisite masterpieces."

Jamal and Youssef are in the same place doing the same exact job. Yet, one is miserable and the other is happy. Why this stark contrast? The difference is in the lens that each person is wearing. Jamal is wearing a lens in which he sees his job as futile and a waste of time. Youssef is wearing a different lens in which he views his occupation as significant because he is part of something grand and beautiful. Although the reality is one, each one of us views it differently based on the lens we choose to wear. If I wear the dark lens of pessimism and negativity, I will see everything around me as ugly and miserable. The father or mother who is at home taking care of the kids, cooking, and doing the laundry will be displeased because he or she views all of these things as burdensome and pointless. The law school student will feel that he is the most miserable person on this earth because he is going through the unending stress of taking exams.

Conversely, if I wear the bright lens of optimism and positivity, I will see things around me as beautiful and uplifting. The same father or mother who is at home taking care of the kids, cooking, and doing the laundry will feel great satisfaction because he or she embraces the role he or she is fulfilling, supporting the family and raising wonderful kids. The law school student will feel proud and accomplished for having the opportunity to receive an education that will secure him a promising future as a legal professional. Which lens will you wear every morning? As you walk out of your house to go to work, school, or run an errand, how will you see the world around you? If you realize you are always displeased and unhappy, it might not be a bad idea to consider changing your prescription.

We do recognize that life is difficult and challenging. We all endure trials and tribulations. We lose a loved one, get laid off, become ill, go out of business, and the list goes on and on. But we must remain aware of the big picture and remind ourselves that we are on a journey. A long-life journey with ups and downs, good days and bad ones. It only helps if we stay hopeful and look for the positive in everything we do. Remembering that God is on our side. Remember that God is always there, He's always listening, and always providing. He promises us that if we call on Him, He will answer.

Taking a moment to reflect on all the blessings we have and not consuming our mind with what we don't, in itself is so key. Our family, security, health, education, job, etc. We cannot take these things for granted. Realizing that we have so much that others around the world can only dream of. Understanding that what we might view as a miserable life is the dream-life of billions of people who are living in destitution and sleeping every night on an empty stomach. Let us embrace what we have. Enjoy the small things. Seize every moment and live with purpose. Reflect on how powerful and capable we are. Look for the extraordinary in the ordinary. And in all of this, remember that as long as we attach ourselves to God, everything will be alright.

TAPPING INTO THE GREAT HOPE

You might reflect and question yourself. How can I view myself as extraordinary when I know I am a sinner? When I spent all my years deliberately disobeying Him? When I committed every wrong, big and small, out there? How can I feel a sense of satisfaction and accomplishment when I know that my record is filled with black marks? The answer is simple. "Say: O my servants who have transgressed against their own souls, do not despair of the mercy of Allah. Surely, Allah forgives all sins. Surely, He is the Forgiving the Merciful."[32] These are the words of God. He is our Great Hope.

See, the reason we are extraordinary is not because we just decided, "That's it, today I'm extraordinary!" It doesn't work like that. We are truly extraordinary because God has created us to be extraordinary. He empowered us with strength, talents, and abilities so that we can do great things. Even when we do not answer our calling and deviate from His course, He has provided us with a wide-open gate to His mercy. Repentance. A gate infinite in size, not subject to time or place. Regardless of the sin or wrong, in terms of quality and quantity, the gate to repentance is always accessible, if we seek it. So how do we seek repentance properly and effectively?

The first thing we have to realize is that God's forgiveness is the greatest blessing we have. It is a product of His mercy and compassion. Just reflect on this for a second. Most people will argue that the heart of a mother has the most compassion and unconditional love. A mother goes out of her way and makes countless sacrifices for the sake of her children. Carrying him for 9 months, sleepless nights, and ongoing concern. Now can you imagine a diso-

---

[32] The Holy Quran, 39:53.

beying and ungrateful child? Someone that defies his mother, disrespects her, mistreats her, and returns all the good she has offered him with bad. In that case, the longer and harsher the mistreatment becomes, the less likely the mother will continue to hold that compassion for her son.

And it can escalate to a point where the mother rejects her son. Worse, even if he seeks forgiveness, she might refuse to accept because of what she endured from him. We know a family in the community where the relationship between the son and his mother became so strained that the mother on her deathbed refused to allow her son to see her and seek her forgiveness. She passed away completely displeased with her son. The point is, that no matter how compassionate the human heart is, whether it is the heart of a mother, father, wife, husband, etc. it is still finite. However, God's mercy is unequivocally infinite. Our Imams inform us that the mercy of God on His servant is more than the heart of a nursing mother on her child. This should be refreshing to us. We should feel optimistic and hopeful. At the same time, we should not take it for granted. This leads us to the next series of questions. What is repentance? How does one seek repentance? What are the conditions?

SEEKING REPENTANCE

Our hearts are filled with goodness. We have desirable qualities such as kindness, compassion, and love. Our innate is good but at times, we stray away from the innate and end up falling into wrong. When one commits the wrong, recognizes it, regrets it, and seeks forgiveness, he is on the path of repentance. If that repentance is sincere and is accepted by God, not only does God forgive us, He conceals our sins. To understand how significant this is, consider this example.

Noor is a 17 year-old junior in high school. She posts an indecent picture of herself on Instagram. After receiving about a hundred likes and two dozen comments, the buzz starts fading away. She starts to reflect on what she did and realizes that the post was wrong and stupid. She rushes to her phone, gets on Instagram, and deletes the picture. Little did she know, one of her classmates downloaded the picture. In that situation, although Noor did realize her wrong, regretted it, attempted to fix it, and possibly even asked for forgiveness, she will not able to conceal her act because others viewed it and one person will have a record of it.

Thus, in that situation, Noor will not be able to completely rectify the situation. However, our relationship with God is not governed by the same dynamic.

God's mercy is so incredibly encompassing, He conceals our sins. Imam Al-Sadiq narrates, "If a person truly repents, God will love him and conceal his sins. Angels will forget the sins they wrote. Body parts will hide the sins they committed. The earth will hide the sins that were committed on it." This further exemplifies the extent of the mercy of God as it relates to repentance. The narration conditions the concealment of the sins on "true repentance." How do we attain that true repentance?

THE CONDITIONS FOR REPENTANCE

Many of us are raised to say *Astaghfurallah* – I ask God forgiveness– when we commit a sin. It is positive to impart this behavior on our kids growing up. Teaching them to be conscious of their actions and accountable when they do wrong is essential. However, what tends to happen with many people is their understanding of repentance becomes limited to uttering these few words. Uttering the statement *Astaghfuralla* becomes a reflex when we commit a wrong. This is a dangerous and distorted understanding of repentance. We say dangerous because if we define repentance as just saying a few words, then we subconsciously start to misuse it and take it lightly. We start to slowly accept doing wrong because in our minds, we can rectify it in an instant by saying the golden words. At that point, not only is our understanding of repentance distorted, we start to undermine an important principle in our faith. By now it is obvious that repentance entails more than just saying *Astaghfurallah*. Imam Ali lays out the conditions of repentance.

Regret what you have done in the past.

Don't be like those that say "I don't regret anything" or "it's all part of the experience." First, that is just flagrant arrogance and we do not need to spend more time discussing arrogance. Remember, you can sit on another table if you're arrogant. Secondly, for those that carry the banner of "it's all part of the experience," that is just immature. How many young people lose their lives, end up in jail, or commit tragedies because they wanted to 'live life to the fullest' or 'experience everything'. Regretting is the first step. It allows us to reflect and contemplate on what we have done. The sense of disappointment and discontent that we have when we regret motivates us to not repeat the same mistake and relive the bitter experience.

Be determined not to return to sin.

We all have spiritual highs and lows. During the Holy Month of Ramadan, we are on a high. We supplicate, read the Quran, and seek nearness to God. During Ashura, we gravitate towards Imam Hussain. We remember his tragedy, revive his principles, and serve in his name. It is only natural that we ascend spiritually during those days. In fact, one of the purposes of these religious seasons is to provide an opportunity for people to refocus on their faith and recharge their spirits. These opportunities are a true blessing that we must invest in for our advancement, not only during the 30 days of Ramadan or 10 days of Ashura, but year round. When we have our lows and do not feel the same sense of connection with God, we need to be on alert and exercise more precaution so that we do not fall into error.

We cannot fall hostage to the vicious cycle of sinning. Consider this example. Mustafa watches obscene movies online. After watching for a while, he feels guilty and asks God for forgiveness. The next day, he is tempted again and watches more videos. An hour later he is regretful and repents... you get the point. A lot of guys have been in Mustafa's shoes. It can be obscene movies, backbiting, cheating, stealing, lying, etc. Yes, we all have temptations. We all sin, repent, and sin again. But we cannot submit to this and accept it as the status quo. No matter how many times we fall down, we need to get back up. We must have the sense of awareness that we will not accept this as our reality. That we will work hard to overcome our desires and hold on to our principles. That we will be inspired by Imam Hussain's will and resolve.

One practical tip that may help all of us is that we need to proactively distance ourselves from temptations that we know will get us in trouble. If I know that sitting in my locked room late at night on my laptop will tempt me to watch that stuff again, then I shouldn't lock my door or go to sleep with the door closed. Alternatively, I might choose to read a book or spend more time with my family in the living room before I go to sleep. If I know that going out with a certain crew will inevitably lead me to smoking, lying, or stealing, then I should avoid that group and find better people to hang out with. We are intelligent and capable of discerning between the environments and people that will promote doing wrong and others that are positive and uplifting.

Pay back people what you owe them.

There are two types of sins. The first sin is a transgression against God. The second sin is a transgression against God and a violation of a person's right. With the latter, God's forgiveness is contingent on rectifying the wrong whether it is via the transgressor seeking forgiveness from the victim, returning something unlawfully possessed, or fulfilling a certain right. The classic example of this type of sin is backbiting.

You attend a Sunday afternoon family barbeque and discussions open up about all sorts of people. If you engage in the discussion and talk negatively about another relative or friend, committing backbiting, you just sinned. A real bad kind of sin too. If you desire to seek repentance, not only do you have to seek it from God, you also have to seek forgiveness from the person who you spoke ill of. Seriously? Yup. We talk about people left and right without giving it a second thought. We need to be careful because the implications are serious.

That is why you find that people preparing to go on the *hajj* pilgrimage usually reach out to the people they know before they travel. They ask them for forgiveness for anything ill they have said or done to them. Furthermore, if you unlawfully took something from someone, you must return it. It's pretty serious. We need to be very cautious before we violate someone else's rights. Who knows if we will ever have an opportunity to ask them for forgiveness. And if we realize we have transgressed against someone else, we need to take immediate action to address them and mend the situation. You really don't know if you'll have the opportunity to do so later on.

Make up any obligatory duties that you have.

As Muslims, we all have obligatory duties. From prayers to pilgrimage, there are specific practices that we need to be engaged in. If we fault in performing these obligations, we need to make them up. If I am a 20-year-old female and I did not start fasting until I was 18, I need to make up fasting for 9 years. If I am a 35-year-old male and I did not start praying until I was 25, I need to make up all the years of missed prayers since I hit the age of maturity. If I made any promises or pledges, I need to fulfill them. These are things we need to take care of when we want to repent.

Therefore, as we learn from Imam Ali, repentance is a multi-step process. It has conditions and requires time and effort. If we commit to following the Imam's prescription and follow the process, God Willing, we will be seeking true and meaningful repentance. Nonetheless, don't be discouraged. Take things one step at a time and keep moving forward.

BEFORE IT'S TOO LATE

Some of us are professional procrastinators. As students, we had our fair share of procrastinating in school. In college, we pulled countless all-nighters studying for exams and writing essays. We might have gotten away with procrastinating and doing well in college. You might get away with procrastinating at work. Although, it is a negative habit and should do away with it both for school and work, at times we still get away with it. However, we will not get away with procrastination when it comes to our relationship with God. The undisputed truth is that we will die one day. If we hold off on seeking repentance and always postpone it for another day, our day might come and catch us off guard. At that point, it'll be too late. Let us not be like those that God describes in the Holy Quran, "Until, when death comes to one of them, he says: 'O my Lord, send me back (to life). That I may do right in that which I have left behind.'"[33] Once the Angel of Death knocks on our doors, we must be ready. There is no second chance. God gives us chances every day. Take advantage of that.

For all of our young friends out there, please do not be misled to believe that "you are too young to repent." That is the wrong way to go. We had friends that died in high school and college. We don't need to remind you that death does not discriminate based on age or health. Every day we wake up in the morning, we should be grateful for another opportunity. Another day. Another chance.

Steve Jobs (1955-2011), the co-founder and CEO of Apple, Inc. delivered a sensational commencement

---

[33] The Holy Quran, 23:99-100.

speech at Stanford University in 2005. He talked about death. "For the past 33 years, I have looked in the mirror every morning and asked myself 'If today were the last day of my life, would I want to do what I am about to do today?' And whenever the answer has been 'No' for too many days in a row, I know I need to change something." When we wake up in the morning, we also need to look into the mirror and ask ourselves the same question. We need to make sure that whatever we are pursuing is meaningful and counts in the eyes of God. If it is not, we ought to reconsider so we do not live our life in vain.

FINAL THOUGHTS

Imam Hussain died so that we may live. He was martyred so we can know right from wrong. He sacrificed so he could preserve the divine guidance we need to achieve our potential and be great. He gave everything he had so we can have everything we need. Today, after 1400 years, we are embarking on our journey inspired by the greatest lessons from Imam Hussain. From him, we can be everything we ought to be, and for that we shall never forget.

You can be anything you want to be. You can be ordinary and you can be great. You can be a dime a dozen or a true gem. At the end of the day the choice is yours. And that is what makes us so amazing. We have the freedom to be whatever we choose. But with that freedom comes great responsibility. We are responsible for ourselves, no one else. We take charge of our lives and we pave the path to our greatness, our mediocrity or our failure. It's in our hands. So even when we fail, even when we fall, even when life knocks us down... it's in our hands to get back up and persevere. No one can weaken you other than yourself. You can be your greatest champion and your greatest obstacle. It is your choice. We believe you will be great, because that is what you were meant to be. We are wired to achieve greatness. It is only when we choose failure that we fail. So don't choose failure. Allow yourself to achieve your potential and persevere. Allow yourself to see greatness and be extraordinary. Remember "... within you lies the greater universe."

ABOUT THE AUTHORS

Jalal Moughania, JD

Growing up in his father's pizzerias, both in Dearborn, MI and Tyre, Lebanon, Jalal Moughania developed a strong work ethic, confidence in his identity, and an unwavering love for pizza. He is now a practicing attorney, author, and public speaker. Moughania has written, translated, and edited over ten books. He currently resides with his wife and daughter in Dearborn Heights, MI.

Abathar Tajaldeen, JD

Abathar Tajaldeen is an attorney and counselor with At Law Group based in Dearborn, Michigan. Coming from a family of immigrants who migrated to the United States in 1997, fleeing Saddam Hussein's persecution, he found a passion in practicing Immigration Law as well as Business Law. He has a background in nonprofit leadership and management, playing an integral role in various national and local community development projects. Tajaldeen currently serves as the Executive Director of the Mainstay Foundation where he focuses on strategic planning, resource management, and community partnerships. He holds a J.D. and B.A. in Economics and Political Science from Wayne State University. Tajaldeen has a passion for teaching and mentoring the youth with personal and professional development.

Mohamed Ali Albodairi, JD

Mohamed Ali Albodairi is Secretary of the Board of Trustees of the Mainstay Foundation. He earned his Juris Doctor degree from Wayne State University Law School and his Bachelors in Political Science and Economics from the University of Michigan. Over the past seven years, he has used his legal and analytical skills to advance communities across the U.S. through the work of various nonprofit organizations. Born in Iraq, Albodairi and his family moved to Syria when he was only 6 months old. In 2001, he settled with his family in the United States. Albodairi is currently a practicing attorney in Dearborn, Michigan.

REFERENCES

The Holy Quran.

Imam Ali. *The Peak of Eloquence*.

Imam Sajjad. *Treatise on Rights*.

Imam Sajjad. *Sahifa Sajjadia*.

Al-Khawarizmi, Al-Muwaffaq ibn Ahmad. *Maqtal Al-Hussain*.

Al-Majlisi, Muhammad Baqir. *Bihar Al-Anwar*.

Al-Tabari, Muhammad ibn Jarir. *Tareekh Al-Tabari*.

Arastu, Rizwan. *God's Emissaries*.

Chamseddine, Muhammad Mahdi. *The Victors of Imam Hussain*.

Ibn Al-Atheer, Muhammad ibn Muhammad. *Al-Kamil fi Al-Tareekh*.

www.ingramcontent.com/pod-product-compliance
Lightning Source LLC
Chambersburg PA
CBHW021222090426
42740CB00006B/335